Extra Joker

EXTRA JOKER

Nicky U. Fox

Copyright © 2002 by Nicky U. Fox.

Library of Congress Number: 2002090657
ISBN: Hardcover   1-4010-4917-6
             Softcover   1-4010-4916-8

All rights reserved. No part of this book may be reproduced or transmitted in any form or by any means, electronic or mechanical, including photocopying, recording, or by any information storage and retrieval system, without permission in writing from the copyright owner.

This book was printed in the United States of America.

To order additional copies of this book, contact:
Xlibris Corporation
1-888-795-4274
www.Xlibris.com
Orders@Xlibris.com

CONTENTS

00/PROLOGUE 13

01/LETTER:
Feb 1942 16

02/CONGRATULATIONS
CAMP GRANT, ILLINOIS
Mar 1942 21

03/THIS IS THE ARMY
CAMP CROWDER, MISSOURI
Mar/Apr 1942 24

04/SOME SORRY SIGNALS
FORT MONMOUTH, NEW JERSEY
Apr/Jul 1942 29

05/MITCHELL MISTAKE
MITCHELL FIELD, NEW YORK
Jul/Aug 1942 38

06/MILLING AROUND
CAMP MILLS, NEW YORK
Aug 1992 39

07/HURRY UP AND WAIT
BAINBRIDGE FIELD, GA
Aug/Sep 1942 42

08/CADET PENNY ARCADE
NASHVILLE, GA.
Sep 1942 48

09/HEY, MISTER
SAN ANTONIO AVIATION CADET CENTER, TEXAS
Sep 1942 52

10/CRAZY CADET CAPERS
KELLY FIELD, TX
Nov/Dec 1942 55

11/LOOK MA, I'M FLYING—OOPS
VICTORY FIELD, VERNON, TEXAS
Nov/Dec 1942 62

12/SECOND TIME AROUND
SAN ANTONIO, TEXAS
Feb/Mar 1943 75

13/MORE OF THE SAME
ELLINGTON FIELD, HOUSTON, TEXAS
Mar/Jun 1943 79

14/AERIAL GUNNERY
HARLINGEN, TEXAS
Jun/Jul 1943 85

15/HOLD THAT HURRICANE
ELLINGTON FIELD, HOUSTON, TEXAS
Jul/Aug 1943 96

16/ADVANCED NAVIGATION
HONDO AAB, TEXAS
AUG/JAN 1944 99

17/WHAT ELSE IS NEW?
WESTOVER FIELD, MASS
Jan/Feb 1944 110

18/OUR NEW CREW
CHARLESTON AAB, WEST VIRGINIA
Mar/Apr 1944 113

19/RADAR AND WAIT
LANGLEY FIELD, VA
Apr/May 1944 123

20/SO LONG, GOODBYE, FAREWELL
MORRISON FIELD, FLA
May 1944 129

21/GOING ABROAD
HITHER AND THITHER
May/Jun 1944 132

22/REPORTING FOR DUTY
FOGGIA, ITALY
June 1944 144

23/EXTRA JOKER ET AL
EUROPE
Jul/Aug, 1944 165

24/SHOT UP
EUROPE
Oct 1944 177

25/SHOT DOWN
EUROPE
Oct 1944 186

26/TYROLEAN TOUR OR ALP!ALP!
LEOBEN, AUSTRIA
OCT 1944 197

27/GORIOUS DEUTSCHES REICH
FRANKFURT/WETZLAR, GERMANY
Oct/Nov 1944 225

28\SORRY SAGAN SAGA
SAGAN, GERMANY
Nov/Jan 1944 244

29/ONE HELLUVA HIKE
TO SPREMBURG, GERMANY
Jan 1945 256

30/NUREMBURG NIGHTMARE
NUREMBURG, GERMANY
Jan/Apr 1945 262

31/BALKING IN BAVARIA
BAVARIAN ALPS
Apr 1945 269

32/TURN AROUND
WURTZBURG, AUSTRIA
Apr 1945 276

33/PARIS IN THE SPRING
PARIS, FRANCE
April 1945 281

34/ITS A BEAUTIFUL DAY IN CHICAGO
   CHICAGO, IL
   Apr/May 1945 287

34/EPILOGUE
   1995 294

DEDICATED TO:

THE IMMEDIATE FAMILY
THE EXTENDED FAMILY
FRIENDS
THE CREW
WALKING PARTNERS
& ZIPPY
(ALL WHO HELPED)

EXTRA JOKER TERMINAL TRIP

00/PROLOGUE

The reader should know that this was written a couple of years after the end of World War II. Registration at the University was done even before formal discharge from the United States Army Air Corps. However, I was refused attendance at the same university previously attended for more than two years at night school because of their quotas. After I received my Bachelor's Degree from a local Catholic University and signed up for a C.P.A. Review Course I became ill and was unable to continue my studies or work. About this time this record was substantially completed in longhand.

In the process of recuperating from the after effects of my experiences in prison camps I started back to work but that's another story. While the writer does not recall exactly how many times the C.P.A. exam was taken, it was far more than most candidates by far. There is the definite recollection, repeated innumerable times then, but almost meaningless now, that it was a major effort to make a pencil erasure during those years. The final completion of this record had to wait until the writer's accounting office was closed and the record was reviewed and edited further. Almost all of this record would not exist if it had not been done earlier (except for the addition of the prologue and epilogue).

Practically all of the names have been changed for reasons of simplicity, security, amusement, protection of privacy etc. This story may be considered fairly typical or completely atypical of G.I.'s (Government Issue/ Soldiers) and the Army Air Corp depending on the readers' backgrounds; although many of the incidents are very specific and hopefully, noteworthy. As noted, a few of the items are not necessarily the immediate experiences of the writer but were viewed by or related to the writer by someone in the Service. Also, they may well represent individual or unofficial viewpoints. As has often been stated by others, the winner in combat is usually the side that makes the least mistakes. Also, it is the writer's hope that our Society is basically more honest than others and therefor in a better position to realize the facts and learn from them.

So that the more genteel are not too often shocked, the phraseology is altered in certain instances. In such cases, the G.I. will have no trouble in substituting the ordinary slanguage used. While the intelligent may never be shocked, there is no insistence on forcing bad language upon others with only the excuse that it is regular Service slanguage.

If, while reading this story, the reader may have the idea that the writer is portrayed unduly as a hero, just take it with a few grains of salt and remember that no one ordinarily portrays themselves as either a dummy or a coward intentionally. But more than anything, the writer does not feel that he accomplished anything more spectacular than many other G.I.'s. The motivation, at certain times, was that certain ideas seemed most practical for the specific situation. Most other soldiers merely did the same thing, although unfortunately, many fared worse but some even better. One can call that fate, or luck or chance if you must label it. The reader may want to keep in mind that the writer did not get to vote on practically any of the events described. But no matter how thin you slice it, as Avigdor Hameiri, the Israeli author of "The Great Madness" and composer/poet etc. and the writer's uncle, also puts it "WAR IS HELL".

That is where training comes in—when you don't have time to think, only to feel and act; you do what is lodged in your mind. If there is nothing there, you can easily become confused and scared. Preparation is the best antidote for initial battle shock with its accompanying strain and gore. When I washed out of pilot training, I felt as though an integral part of my life had been cut out. Yesterday it was the biggest thing in my life and today it did not exist. Yet until I left, I hung around the flight line just watching.

On the one hand I have tried to keep the personalities that are presented as stable/constant so that the reader will not be confused. However, on the other hand, since the writer was in so many different camps, and the other soldiers very rarely accompanied the changes in location, therefore many different names/people are mentioned. While it is felt that the names are not particularly important, there is no question that the people/soldiers are. Since the Services severely restricted Blacks' activities at that time, we did not intermingle, except for minor exceptions such as at Harlingen. But at San Antonio when we discussed/argued about race and the writer was called a "nigger lover"(and being Jewish) and aware of such blind prejudices, it was considered more of a compliment than an insult. However, hopefully, a more correct description would be a respecter of humanity. The religions and origins of others are mostly unknown because it was never felt that this was important. The particular persons interactions, socially and otherwise, are however important. For those very few that may still be around, and may recognize one or more of the events as related: "Hi".

01/LETTER: FEB 1942

(DEAR MR. ANTHONY: (From one of the most popular ANSWER MAN radio programs of the Forties. I loved it when the assistants would say: "I have a Lady,
Doctor" when there were so few lady doctors in the real world.))
"D. GOLDENBOY, LT. (JG) USN (RET.)
U.S.NAVY RECRUITING STATION
CHICAGO, ILLINOIS
WHAT WOULD YOU DO?
I am 23 years old, have had two and a half years of college, am in perfect health (eyes 20/15), with an official (Navy) I.Q. of 93/100 and without any bad habits.

Last summer I made application to become a third class yeoman in the Naval Intelligence Reserve (V-4 classification). Then my draft board saw fit to permit me to finish my study of Accounting; going to night school and taking the C.P.A. Examination in May 1942. I then requested, by letter, that the Naval Reserve should please hold my application open until May. Some months later, I received a form letter stating that my qualifications were insufficient. I was later told, upon inquiry, that the most probable reason I was refused, was because I didn't know shorthand.

About a month ago, I was cramming, my last three subjects

in Accounting, when I was notified that I was to be reclassified from 2A deferment.

I then investigated all possible entrances into the service.

I dropped the C.P.A. Review which I could not continue until May. On Jan 21 I applied at the Naval Armory for the midshipman school (V-7 classification). That evening I received notice to report for my first physical exam on the 26th. On the 23rd I drove to Urbana after having my credits forwarded accordingly.

On Feb 5th I sold my car at quite a loss. I stopped at the Naval Armory to drop off my birth certificate and three letters of recommendation.

I was told that the Armory's quota was too close to being filled for me to have a chance waiting for the physical exam. scheduled on Feb. 12th. However, he read the letters and said I would still have a chance at the U.S. Courthouse.

When I got to the Courthouse, I was seated quite informally, interrupting the Ensign having his coffee. I was in a bit of a hurry and informed the Ensign of that indirectly. He asked me a few questions and the interview was over.

The next day I registered at Illinois. I had thus far, spent better than one hundred dollars in expenses to qualify for V-7. About six days later I received word that my application had been refused. The Ensign said that I had not impressed him as having the necessary qualities of leadership. Which was in direct contrast to my letters of recommendation.

On Feb. 12, I returned to see the Ensign, who refused to change his opinion because he wasn't sure.

I then went to the Flight Selection Board. After a preliminary physical I was told to come back. The next day I was interviewed. When the interviewing officer learned that I had been refused entrance into V-7 and had not flown (or ridden) in an airplane, he said he could get better qualified men. (I told him I could pass any test he gave me and he agreed).

That made three different times I was refused entrance into the Navy . . .

Both interviewers said that their opinion was only an estimation. A large percentage that they pass still do not reach the goal. However, I object to being sentenced without a fair trial. That is what it amounts to.

But that is not the whole story. Following are a few miscellaneous items to help judge:

I have participated in neighborhood athletics as far back as I can remember. I can skate, run, swim, fence etc. reasonably well. I can box, and drive (motorcycle, bicycle, auto) exceptionally well.

In my first year in high school I was a volunteer afterschool teacher in Algebra to backward students. In my last year in high school I entered the intramural Golden Gloves Tourney, winning in my division. My second time on a motorcycle I drove. Have been a member of A.Z.A, consisting of about 60 fellows, under 21. I later became an Advisor, resigning when I made the first application in the Naval Intelligence Reserve. I also refused the offer of the D.B.C. Director to become a paid group advisor, for the same reason.

I have worked quite steadily since my third year of high school. Last week I took leave of Manufacturing Co. as a cost accountant, presumably to join the Naval Reserve.

Within the next three days I will have had an airplane ride.

But it won't be to settle anything, just so I can say that I have had one.

The courses that still are assumedly open are:
Enlistment —Army Air Corps
  —Navy Radar Man (my bro is in right now)
  —V-6 Yeoman
Selective Service

There is the situation, to become incensed at it and despondent, would be to prostitute my ability and shirk my duty to my country and family. My conscience is still clear.

Sincerely yours
(Sig)"

I only did one thing with that letter that was irrelevant, unimportant and unnecessary—I mailed it. Period. Never heard another thing about it. So I spent a couple of weeks in the city without a car. Which I didn't like in addition to paying rent at three different addresses. Then I figured I'd give the Army a chance. They asked me the twenty-one dollar question and I was in like Flynn (A private earned twenty-one dollars per month in 1942 upon induction/ shades of Flynn, the movie actor/lover).

02/CONGRATULATIONS CAMP GRANT, ILLINOIS MAR 1942

I could have gone into the Navy with our youngest brother, Will, but by then I did not care for the Navy. He had enlisted in January. The older brother, Burns, enlisted the same week that I was drafted. The oldest brother, Saul, was married.

Those preliminary examinations for the draft were not too bad. The first time we were all local fellows. We were all a little nervous amidst such strange goings-on. They asked a bunch of silly questions about bed-wetting, insanity, homicidal tendencies, did we like girls etc.. etc. As if we would admit such things anyway. Then we took a physical exam. Of course, you have all heard of some guys, like the one who drank a bottle of vinegar, to eat his stomach out so that he would not be drafted. Or the fellows that kept taking aspirins before the exam and the doctors could not understand what made their hearts act up. Then they put one in the hospital for observation, where he could not get any aspirin. Then he was in and his heart must have beat pretty fast after that.

So there I stood, Serial Number 1213, 772 on the list at the Draft Board #126 at 939 N. Kedzie, at 14:30 hours on March 10, 1941 with a score of other draftees. The Bored Chairman gave us a spiel. We should be proud that we had been especially selected amongst all the citizens available and were in excellent physical condition. that we were going out to do battle for our glorious country which had every reason to be proud of us and that none of our past histories was besmirched by a criminal record. I looked around but after all no one knew that there were two warrants out for my arrest—for traffic violations. But the judge was very understanding. He had two sons in the service and dismissed the charges.

1. Our indoctrination went pretty fast. We were given to understand that if we stepped out of line on the way to our first camp, that we were committing a Federal offense. The train from Chicago sped along at well over ten miles per hour—later we found that this was good speed for a G.I. Troop Train. Nobody knew what to expect so we exchanged confidences trying to impress each other with our own importance.

The food at Camp Grant (about forty miles west of Chicago) was very good. Not only that, we just got in line and kept walking until we got served. How eagerly I always looked for a similar chow line after that, before I finally realized it must have been an accident. Everything, particularly shipping lists were in a high state of flux. Anybody who remained for just a day or two was really an old-timer. They possessed the know-how for washing windows, mopping floors etc. Besides which they were very much imbued with the community spirit to break us feather merchants in properly. Especially when they were the straw bosses. But we were so ignorant of so many things that we made very eager pupils.

We were sworn in 11 March 1942, just one week after my 23rd birthday. Then we took our Army Classification tests. Because I had done the Navy examination in half the time and gotten a good mark, I figured I would have plenty of time for the Army General Classification Test. Then I only finished 124 of 150 questions and got a grade of 134 out of a possible 160. I always figured I could do much better on a retake but I didn't want to risk getting a lower mark.

I got 145 out of 150 questions on the Mechanical Aptitude Test. Then I took a typing test and got 35 wpm. I didn't know they wouldn't count the mistakes which I had stopped to erase. We then got psychological interviews. I was a little worried because it took well over an hour. Also, the psychologist might have thought as little of me as I did of him. Then we signed up for life insurance as if we had a choice.

We got our first Army passes Friday night and went right into town. Our uniforms didn't create quite the stir that we subconsciously hoped and looked for. We very excitedly explored the new "INS" that our uniform gave us. We made the rounds of all the two U.S.O.'s in town before returning to camp. It was jolly good sport meeting girls informally and becoming acquainted without feeling it was "improper".

We had figured out practically all the details and angles of getting a bus chartered to take us back to Chicago for our first "weekend" pass. Then we found out that the proverb now went: "The soldier proposes and the Army disposes", and talked about it on the train the next day, Saturday, going South. In conversation on the train I noticed that many of the fellows had not asked for the same thing that I had. So I took a poll and there seemed to be a pretty even division between those asking for the Signal Corps and those asking for the Air Corps. Only we were all going to the same place and it obviously wasn't going to please everyone.

03/THIS IS THE ARMY CAMP CROWDER, MISSOURI MAR/APR 1942

We arrived at the Signal Corps Camp in the morning. So the ones that had asked for the Signal Corps got what they wanted. Upon investigating the activity at the Mess hall near the Company area our worst fears were realized. It was having a Grand Opening at dinner time. And sure enough, we learned what the Army chow really was like almost as fast as the cooks did. It was lucky that we had strong stomachs from civilian life. One of the entrees they served was ham. Since a lot of the fellows in the group were Jewish they had not eaten ham before and originally thought it was a form of corned beef. I don't know if I did my "lantsmen" a favor by correctly identifying the ham. Here most of us first learned to "goof off". The new mess non-coms (Non-Commissioned Officers) tried to keep us busy straight through on K.P. But it was much better to find any easy task and look busy than have the cooks order us a hard one.

The Camp was so new that a number of girls set up shop in the newly evacuated farmhouses that hadn't yet been demolished and still decorated the otherwise empty fields. That is, they were in business only until they got a little too much free advertising. We were housed in new but otherwise regular Army barracks. I had a corner of the second floor. Connecting my portable radio where everyone could hear it was generally appreciated. However, there was a preponderance of hillbilly music which grated on a few nerves. The radio had to be shelved for Saturday morning inspections.

On the shelves, was a conglomeration of bottled concoctions. You know, powders, perfumes and such. When I used to see the Junque that my two sisters kept in the medicine cabinet at home I used to wonder what they did with it all. Now, by comparison, I began to wonder how they had gotten by with so little.

The Camp didn't hold weekend classes. Just having gotten into the Service we were quarantined for two weeks. So the first time that we could we went for a walk to look at the field, which was supposed to be immense. We walked to the main highway and then along it. A man came by in a station wagon and told us to hop in. Then and there we decided we were going to town. We didn't just go to town. Mr. Nashua was a Southern Gentleman and owned all two of the theatres in Neosho. He took us for a very leisurely and comfortable tour of the vicinity, ending up at his residence just outside of town. I thought that was pretty fast. Not even in the Service a week and AWOL (Absent Without Official Leave) already. But of course, it was all on the Q.T.(Quiet).

A PFC (Private, First Class) was a little tin god. All you had to do was ask him. We got instructions on how to pack. For a new bunch of inductees, we sure had a lot of suggestions on how to improve the standard Army pack. After two-thirds of the period was over the instructor finally told us that he didn't give a good g-d-damn how we thought it should be packed. That he was showing us the Army way and that was the way we were going to do it so we might as well learn it and right away.

Here we took our basic training. Daily drill. What fun? We drilled with G.I. shoes, in fatigues, with packs, with picks and shovels, with the Lieutenants, Sergeants, Corporals and Privates. We did close order drill, we did squad drill, we did Company drill. Maybe you think we got bored from drilling. We eventually all learned to put the same foot out in front at the same time. After ten hours of drill you knew enough to step out and tell the beginners how to do it. Then they let a few of us step out and give commands to the others.

We went to school and learned to make a Signal Corps splice (to connect wires) and how to use a pair of pliers. In the evening, after school and after drill, writing a letter home or getting equipment ready for the morrow seemed to require effort above and beyond the call of duty. Here we first became acquainted with the Sex Morality Lectures. The Medical Corps would show movies of actual instances of venereal diseases and a good many of the fellows felt sick the first time and then hated to go to subsequent showings. They showed how to be careful—which was important. Then the Chaplain took over and tried to convince the fellows of the advantages of continence. Most of them spoke in ordinary language to meet the fellows on their level. These were the ones that got the most attention.

This camp must have been where that remark originated: "That it's just a coincidence when the road turns the same way that the car does". The jeeps and command cars ran riot through the Company area. But then it was hard to tell which was road and which was not. When it rained, we walked through ankle deep mud. Not ordinary mud, but red muck. With superior adhering qualities. Since we had to G.I. (Clean and scrub) the barracks for SMI (Saturday Morning Inspection) we had to clean off our shoes before we went inside. Of course, when it didn't rain, the sun shone like blazes. Everything would dry up, including the people. The dust filled the air so much that we almost welcomed gas mask drill so we could breathe clear air.

We were given aptitude tests for code and electricity. I flunked the code, but got a pretty good mark on the electrical aptitude—34 out of 50. We then had additional interviews. I was told with my background I wouldn't learn anything as a Company Clerk and that I should go to school as a radio technician. Since the radio school at Crowder wasn't going to open till after July I was marked for shipment to the main Signal Corps field at Ft. Monmouth, New Jersey.

After completing four weeks of basic training so that our clothes didn't have the Q.M. (Quarter Master/Warehouse) smell nor the barracks bag creases it was time to ship out. The routing was right through Chicago, happy day. With a three hour stopover, wonderful. Only we stood packed and assembled and waited for the train for four hours. In that four hours there were enough rumors passing around, concerning what was happening and what was going to happen, to fill a book. The train got to Chicago six hours late. All the way to the City we'd been bragging about "Our Home Town". So what happened. First, no time off for sight-seeing or visiting. Second, a good many of us could pick out the houses where we lived as the train went along Grand Avenue.

Thirdly, we went through by way of the back door—the rail yards, the stock yards, the poor sections etc. Fourth, we stopped at 95th street and no one was allowed to make phone calls or move more than a hundred feet from the train while it was being checked. We were three miles from my sister's house. After calling from Camp Grant, Il. and calling from Camp Crowder, Mo.—now no calls were allowed. Of course, a handful of fellows, well, three anyway, went about a half block and used a phone booth there, but no one knew for sure when the train would move out. Of course, we braggers from Chicago took quite a razzing from the rest of the men.

04/SOME SORRY SIGNALS FORT MONMOUTH, NEW JERSEY APR/JUL 1942

At the new camp we were told that the Signal Corps rated next to the Air Corps. Radio repair rated best in the Signal Corps. So we were to be given class A passes and to be treated like men. We could leave the field anytime we were off duty (or appeared to be).

They had two school shifts because of the crowded conditions. Luckily our Company had the good one. They crowded almost 200 men to a barracks floor, gave us seats, a book on radio engineering and told us to study. The book was a good review for a radio engineer. Even electronic specialists who came through used to argue with the school about some of the things in the book. I hate to say that the course was bad but it was even worse than that. We were supposed to take an examination on each chapter in about a day and a half. The hardest job was just to stay awake. It was during the warm summer months and we had to be in full uniform, as always. But they did concede finally, to let us wear fatigues to school so that we wouldn't keep our two khaki uniforms dirty all the time. If anyone fell asleep he was made to stand up until someone else was found dozing off. Then the new person would take over. This custom prevailed all through radio theory. A few of the fellows finally got

P.O.'d(Pissed Off) and convinced the Officer in charge that we should have lectures on the material. But it was too late for us.

I guess I just didn't like the way they didn't teach. Anyone who memorized the book and got a good grade could become a teacher after finishing the course. I got tired of confusing the instructors with my questions. It got to the point where I would approach an instructor with two questions. The first one would be what I really wanted to know. When the instructor started rambling too much in unfamiliar territory I asked the second question that was extremely simple. The instructor could then answer that easily and I could go back and sit down again. The instructors were nice fellows who didn't seem to mind fooling the students rather than get shipped out. Only the non-coms in charge of the last line of instructors were really radio men. They told us that when we finished the course we would be the guys who were apprentices and carry the radios for the experienced mechanics. That's when I started seriously thinking of being a Flying Cadet.

One of the fellows received a commission directly so that he could go to England to study Electronics. He had already finished college. The Company really buzzed with the news when his orders came through. He had to immediately move into the Officers' Quarters; he could no longer associate with the enlisted men.

While practicing on the punching bags and stuff, there was another fellow taking turns with me. He had a build that would look good on an Atlas. My build may not have been too bad but his was far, far more developed. He suggested putting on the gloves for a little practice. We began exchanging blows thick and fast. This went on for a few days and I enjoyed it immensely. I was very careful to see that he couldn't get through my guard while every once in a while I would get through his guard. About the fourth day when we were in the ring he apparently became unhappy at not getting through as much as I and he started rushing me. When I felt the ropes against my back I waited as usual with my guard up until he started backing off, as was our custom. Only this time as I relaxed I could see him start a hard right, with his weight behind it, landing smack on the chest muscle in front of my heart. With the start of the blow I tried to bring my hands back up and I only succeeded in having him hit my outstretched arm with his head. His blow really shook me up and must have shown in the pained expression on my face. Even as I gritted my teeth I lunged forward for revenge. But he back-pedaled very fast, holding both gloves out and saying: "That's enough for today." It was just supposed to be a friendly encounter so that was that. Only whenever I went to the gym after that he was never there.

    I then drew K.P. and strained the same muscle or ligament further and went on sick call. Doctor Dean told me to exhale fully. Which I very trustingly did. My chest was then confined in a huge adhesive corset. It took two days before I could draw a full deep breath. After my chest was X-rayed I was told to come back in five days to find out if I had any broken ribs. By that time chunks of skin had been pulled out of place by the tape. This was further aggravated when it came time to remove the adhesive tape and more skin was lost but at least there were no other problems.

    We seemed to have hit New Jersey in the midst of their largest precipitation and highest humidity. Every morning I could see the condensation on the inside of my waterproof watch. Also, just about every morning we had to practically wring out our clothes to put them on. Yet there was a resident layer of dust in our tent. You know how when fellows put their slacks on in the morning the second leg is dropped on the floor. I offered to clean out the tent if no one disturbed the tent until I was all through. I got all the dust swept and piled in the last one-fifth of the floor area around the door. But it seemed that the men could wait no longer. After the door was opened and closed about eight times I stamped out disgustedly and gave it up as a bad job. And the gigs continued.

The Special Services Officer was quite active and we had lots of talent out to the field hot from New York City. We enjoyed Porgy and Bess even though it was almost rained out. Also Kay Kayser showed and contributed a large asbestos curtain for the outdoor theatre. They held a show strictly for G.I. talent. I had previously submitted my name for acting and was asked to perform. Not having any skit I recited a comic poem: "Please Give Your Dog A Decent Name". With the unfamiliar spotlight on me, I couldn't really see the audience and came through pretty poorly although my name appeared in the paper. But some of the fellows like Larry went on to a program in Camp with Irving Berlin and Eddie Cantor and thence to "This Is the Army". I had seen Irving Berlin in person at the Chicago Stadium at the Tribune Show so the voice of the creator of so many beautiful songs was no surprise. I volunteered as a stage hand for Eddie Cantor's show so that I could get a closer look at him. His Roman Scandals was the only picture I ever saw three times. I'd only glimpsed him in the elevator at the Covenant Club in Chicago. But here he had brought all those beautiful girls from his New York show which had been closed by his Doctor's orders.

At one of the dances in Asbury Park I had my eye on one girl who was being squired by a Lt. I talked Blackie into us walking her and her girl friend home. I never saw either of them again but a couple of years later I found out that Blackie had married that girl he had walked home.

I think Adam was from Oklahoma. He'd always been a big man with the women. We took off for New York and were walking around Times Square when we chanced to meet a couple of girls. They expected to take the two o'clock train back to New Jersey. We all took a cab to Leon and Eddy's and I figured it was going to be an expensive evening. It turned out that Leon and Eddy had served in the last war (WW1). As soon as we two privates got at the end of the line we were promoted to the head of the line. Getting in right away we sat at the bar just in time for the floor show. All the while Adam was busy trying to convince his doll that she should miss the train. My companion and I enjoyed the excellent floor show. But what I particularly liked was that the bartender practically ignored us. One drink lasted us the whole evening. Felt like a real big shot at Leon and Eddy's being treated with such respect. Of course I knew it was just the uniform. To watch Adam and his doll you would have thought that they knew each other forever and were deeply in love. My companion and I engaged in interesting conversation and had a very good time. At two A.M. we kissed the girls goodbye in the station and retired to our hotel.

The next day we went to Coney Island. This was the first time in the Army that I got a soda to compare with the ones in Chicago. We had hot dogs and popcorn and tried the rides and the shooting galleries. Only one of the rides seemed rougher than

Riverview's in Chicago. There were loads of girls there but of course we had to return that night to Camp so . . .

On one of the trips to New York, Adam and I were to meet or leave word at the Pennsylvania Station U.S.O. on the way back to Camp for Timmy, who was from the east side of Chicago. When Adam and I came through the U.S.O. I spotted one of the loveliest dolls it has ever been my pleasure to see. I went right up to her and said: "When Timmy comes through here, tell him that Adam and Nick have gone". She was quite flabbergasted and asked: "How do you know that Timmy will ask me about you?" But I had the utmost faith in Timmy and I assured her that if Timmy ever saw her he'd have to think of something to talk to her about. The elderly (over 25) hostess standing next to her understood the compliment but I don't think that beautiful doll did even after we left. Timmy, meanwhile, had gone to see his aunt and had been pretty tired when he got on the subway. As it turned out, he fell asleep on the train and missed his transfer point. When he awoke at the end of the line he started back toward the transfer point. Only he fell asleep again and went to the other end of the line. The next time he made the transfer and then repeated the process. Instead of arriving at his aunt's to sleep there he arrived in time for breakfast. He didn't stop to ask for us at the U.S.O. either.

After being in three months we were eligible for OCS. If one could stand the strain of the multitudinous detail on the questionnaire as well as the infinite revision during the interim of filling it out and checking it at headquarters; then you dragged out the pins and needles to wait on while they checked you off for an interview. Just because I got turned down, I don't want you to think that I'm prejudiced but it seemed that they took every single slacker in our Company. One of those accepted had turned out for drill twice in two months. After the first week he rightly figured that he was so far ahead of the game that he could afford to be punished and still come out ahead. But, of course, he was never caught or punished. I got turned down because of a lack of leadership and lack of mechanical aptitude. The Mechanical Aptitude test grade of 140 out of 150 appeared nowhere on the application. Evidently nobody bothered about such details. The First Sgt. then tried to get me to drill the others for his own curiosity but I left before he got the chance.

One of the things that must have affected my O.C.S. application was that I admitted being rejected by the Navy. I knew that it could be checked; just as much as I knew that it would not be. But 2nd Lt. Tish saw that and it undoubtedly influenced him in giving me a character recommendation of "good". Anything under excellent was worthless. Also my marks in radio school were getting bad. But I wasn't learning radio theory. After three years of hobnobbing with first rate radio engineers, I at least had an idea of what should be gotten out of the course. For instance, I attempted to figure out the dynamic tube characteristics to determine change in plate current corresponding to change in grid current. But I couldn't get anyone there to help me.

Using the same three letters of recommendation I applied for Cadet training. Now that Lt. Cody was back I got an excellent character rating but I didn't fully appreciate the difference at the time. But everyone appreciated the change in the mess situation when Lt. Cody got back. As K.P.'s we worked our tails off. But those on K.P. punishment detail took it easier than even the cooks. While 2nd Lt. Dale was in charge he tried to make a good impression with the help and eased up on the cooks etc. Under

Lt. Cody our mess hall kept winning or tieing for the field inspections.

In order to qualify for the Aviation Cadets I had to take examinations at Fort Dix, N.J. The Company Clerk gave me the address of a friend of his, George, so that I could get a bunk for the night.

At Fort Dix I started looking for K Company and friend and nobody had even heard about it. So I just walked and walked. The last guy I asked about it lived next door to it, about a hundred feet away and he had no idea as to its location. Luckily I stumbled on it. Going into one of the barracks I asked for George. The Corporal under him told me that George was back in Tennessee. What did I want to see him about? Thus it came out about the Cadet examinations. These fellows there thought that was pretty hot stuff. This Corporal was a very obliging chap and took me to the mess hall and got me fed. Then back to the barracks to find me an empty bunk. He had to ask the other soldiers who were A.W.O.L., how long, and when they were expected back. The Company was expected to ship out overseas soon and no leaves had been granted for last minute visits. So the fellows left on their own initiative.

About forty fellows took the screening test of 150 questions. I took the full three hours feeling the full effect of my cold. We had to get 80 right to pass, which most of us did. Upon finishing I felt sure that I had flunked but I came out with a 121. Having only one day to complete everything I next took a 6-3 physical. That's different from the draft board examination where they just see if you're there. This one required some movement. Then I had to wait for the interview with the Board.

The Board turned out to be a mild mannered Captain who

asked such questions as: "Could you make a speech before 500 men?" To which I answered: "I could if I had something to talk about". "Can you identify any airplanes?" "No. But I can learn just as I did with cars". He suggested that I start learning immediately and gave me the names of a few magazines.

Not desiring to be rejected again like the previous Board interviews, this being the one that I really desired, I had reviewed the most likely questions and answers. I left in a happier frame of mind feeling quite certain from the Captain's instructions that I'd been accepted.

Back at Ft. Monmouth, school attendance was still required even after they got word that I was alerted for shipping. On the last test I took I had to go back to the instructor because I had gotten a failing mark. I finally was able to show and convince the instructor that my answer was correct even if it didn't agree with the book. He promised to change the record. Unfortunately, he didn't and I still got a failing grade. I goofed off plenty then and didn't really bother with radio theory anymore. Being careful not to sign out when I left the post or when I returned.

05/MITCHELL MISTAKE MITCHELL FIELD, NEW YORK JUL/AUG 1942

My train ticket took me to Hempstead, N.Y. I found a bus to take me to Camp and paid my fare. I guess the Army didn't know about it because technically I should have called up the nearest Army post and let them take care of the transportation. As a private I could do no wrong by refusing to think for myself. But I thought it best not to make any fuss. Arriving at Mitchell Field in the afternoon I reported to the new arrivals' barracks. Then I talked to one of the E.M. at the orderly room and no one was sure of what I was supposed to do.

My orders read to report to the C.O. at Mitchell Field, which is customary for orders. But each field has someone in charge of the reception detail. I had no desire to bother the C.O. who didn't even know that I existed and that was okay by me. The E.M. finally referred me to the Sgt. Major who determined that I did not belong at Mitchell Field proper but at Camp Mills. But I had a bed there for that night.

I reported to Camp Mills the next morning.

06/MILLING AROUND CAMP MILLS, NEW YORK AUG 1992

I arrived at Camp Mills on Saturday morning 1 August, reported to the Orderly Room and requested a weekend pass. That confused everyone for a while before it was refused. I can't say that I was surprised or disappointed. Everyone there was waiting to ship out. The Camp had formerly been used for a crack infantry outfit and we used the same tents. Since everyone in Camp was just waiting, the biggest thing was the duty roster. One just reeled and rotated from K.P. to guard duty, to special detail and back again. KP there was something to be dreaded. The hours were from 0400 to 2100 and not much if any time off, to go to the john and such. It was one mess hall for hundreds and hundreds of cadet candidates. It took either pull or brains or luck or all to stay off any undesirable activity for any length of time. Passes were only issued to the lucky ones.

Early Sunday morning they got up a volunteer detail and offered over-night passes to New York. So in the worst Army tradition, I volunteered. We went to the gym and moved some seats around and collected our passes. Blackie, my friend from Chicago, wasn't at the USO but there were some nice girls. I still liked to go to New York City even if it was only to just leave Camp and walk around where there were still lots of civilians.

To kill time and keep out of sight I started going to the gym at Mitchell Field and working out. Then I saw Gary about getting on the boxing team, figuring that we would stick around for some time. I punched the big bag for him and he asked if I would be ready by Friday. I didn't think that I was in that good condition and would prefer to wait a week. There were some other men around when I told him I was staying at Camp Mills. One of the others then remarked that I must be with that "Suicide Group".

In the week that I was at Camp Mills I went to New York two more times and went out to parties twice. One of them was a block party, in a suburb, sponsored by the Legion, I think. We all had a very good time. The dancing was interrupted only once for speeches and a Major stood up and thanked the sponsors on behalf of the soldiers. He very obviously had never had any cheer leading experience. Winding up his thank you speech he said that the soldiers would now give a cheer to prove their appreciation. So we all waited for the signal to cheer—but there wasn't any. Only silence, quiet and embarrassing silence followed his announcement. The Major ended up very lamely saying that the soldiers didn't feel like cheering. But we all did want to cheer only everyone was afraid of doing it solo.

Another party was at a very exclusive night club or roadhouse. It wasn't near any big city. We again had G.I. transportation, fifteen or more bodies to a 6x6 truck. That's one of those Army vehicles that travels up and down and sideways almost as much as it does forward. If the top is off/up everyone runs for the front seats. When the top is on/down the rear seats get all the fresh air. Unless it is on a dusty road where the turbulence sucks the dust right in the back of the truck. Then your hair turns gray.

They had a number of parlor games at this club and free

drinks to the men in uniform. One of the games was to have a dozen men line up with materials for womens' hats. They were given about five minutes to fashion some creation that a dame might conceivably place on her dome. It was a scream. After they started the eliminations on that one it became obvious that the best hat alone was not going to win. The strut around the room to display the object de art had to be plenty sexy too. I suspect that the fellows enjoyed that one more than the girls that originated the idea.

I was in the same tent with Herman, who'd just been voted the best short story writer of the year. He had contributed regularly to Esquire and others in that class. So I really wasn't that exposed to his writings. I listened attentively to his tales of drinking champagne cocktails in the afternoons etc. He was a more than average quiet fellow otherwise and he talked to me far more than any of the others. So his remark to me: "You're a good kid but you talk too much" wasn't as surprising as it might have been. He was waiting for a shipment as a cadet candidate while others were just holdovers hoping for permanent assignment to Mitchell Field.

As soon as we got orders to leave Camp Mills, I asked to leave the Post so that I could get my uniform from the cleaners in town. It would have taken about twenty-five minutes to do. After waiting over five hours, we shipped out with my uniform still in the cleaners. Unfortunately, this was to happen more than a half dozen times.

07/HURRY UP AND WAIT BAINBRIDGE FIELD, GA AUG/SEP 1942

So we wound up getting off the train in the deep South. It was before daybreak that we pulled up on the siding near the town. One by one, the fellows woke up. After almost everyone was awake the Lt. got up and started to see about getting transportation for us. We finally got transportation to the Camp. It turned out that we weren't particularly expected yet. However, they split up all the Cadet Candidates and assigned about twenty to each squadron there. We did offer to turn around and go back to civilization but it was no go. The Camp was a basic flying training field and had been in operation for over three months.

By then we knew we were not going to pre-flight but we still did not know what to expect. So, early in the afternoon, the C.O. gathered all the hopefuls together in front of the orderly room and explained that we were just there as fill-ins and would have to do anything we were told. It wasn't a particularly long talk. But it sure seemed long. He had no sooner started talking then he was ceaselessly brushing the fleas away from his face. At first we laughed because it looked so funny. But we joined him one by one and there we all stood; waving our hands back and forth in a fruitless endeavor to rid ourselves of the winged pests.

It was a terrible discrimination to be shipped out to what we thought was some hole in the States while so many others experienced no such inconvenience in going straight through to Cadet training. We were just so much excess baggage hanging around. They gave us the odd jobs to do. They put us on all duty rosters. We were beginning to feel like forgotten men. After a few talks with the Cadets who were taking basic flying training we learned that sooner or later, we too would be recalled and started on active Cadet training.

We were allowed a pass only every other day. What was required was that fifty percent squadron strength remain on the field at all times, in case of fire or other emergency. The town wasn't a big town.

After I got on talking terms with one of the local girls I was told some very interesting things about the town and folk. Like they still called Northerners: "Damnyankees". The mothers had forbidden the daughters to go out with any of the Damnyankee soldiers. She also said that only four months ago, or a month before the Camp had been opened, the Confederate flag had been removed from the City Hall Building. One of the soldiers started a riot in a local tavern. After over-imbibing he began to sing: "Marching Through Georgia". It obviously went over like a lead balloon. I didn't hear if he had a good voice or not—as if that would have made any difference.

The local theatre was even smaller than our neighborhood show in Chicago. I wrote my sisters that I was catching up on all the movies that I had missed in the last couple of years. They always had a cowboy picture on Saturday. Public entertainment was limited to the theatre and the taverns, which did a lively business. The first week there we considered the girls' Southern accent just too cute for words and we engaged the girls in conversation at every opportunity. But one time, while a half dozen of us were talking to two local female cyclists, one of our buddies, across the street, exclaimed that he was talking to a girl from the North. I guess we must have been South long enough to get homesick because we hot-footed it across the street to hear the Northern girl talk. That is, all except Jason, who later dated one of the cyclists.

There was a lot of talk about getting a USO club there but it never happened in the short time that we were there. The female situation at best, was not very good. It got to the point where they posted a notice on the bulletin board that everyone read with quite a bit of amusement. It was to the effect that: "None of the white soldiers were to be seen in the company of Negro girls".

We learned a lot from the Cadets flying from the field even though some of it wasn't true. They said that nobody gets washed out in basic. Either they killed themselves or asked to get out. The fellows that did wash out seemed heart-broken. The G.I.'s told us that it was no disgrace to wash out. That anyone who had qualified as an Aviation Cadet had plenty of reason to be proud. But we secretly felt that it was a terrible thing to wash out, even then.

The local G.I.'s resented us until they found out that we weren't assigned and therefore couldn't get any ratings to compete with them. Still there was some friction. On the surface it was unaccountable. Practically everyone of us had been in the Army before volunteering for the Cadets. But the fact that we had qualified apparently represented an unforgivable gap. I got stuck with K.P. The work inside was not at all conducive to pleasure. One of the Corporals was bucking for K.P. pusher and first cook. No one appreciated his eagerness. We mopped the floor with so much water that the new floorboards buckled.

Working outside on the G.I. cans used for washing the mess kits was much more pleasant and independent. The washline was very long and often meant waiting as much as 45 minutes, which gave rise to a lot of beefing. When I changed the arrangement of the cans and the lines everyone got through in about five minutes. But in order to sell the new system I had to become a "barker" and explain until everyone understood. The Mess Sgt. okayed the operation. But the Adj., who was the Assistant Mess Officer, "ate me out" when he discovered the change. He then told the Mess Sgt. who then expressed his disapproval and ordered that the previous method with one long line be used. Then the Mess Capt. came around and it was all explained to him. Given full authority then, the change came back to stay with the five minute lines. It got to be such a joke that the men would walk up and say: "How do we do it today, Nick?" The Mess Adj. wasn't pleased at all. Do you think that is the reason I got a character classification on my record as "Unknown"?

Later the Adj. and I had a little talk about a job in the Service Department. He said that in view of my civilian background he was going to give me an opportunity to get some really excellent experience. But if there was the least little complaint about me or the work, I would be yanked back to the onerous jobs again. Modest me, I told him that I never had any complaints about my work. He said that he could think of a few himself. His remark wasn't challenged. I went over to see what the wonderful opportunity was about. The Sgt. who explained the system was very nice. So I very gently told him a few things about the system that he didn't tell me. After that he didn't give me any more instructions. We then got along real fine. I liked to work with him. Course, there wasn't much to do. He asked me to type up some "Poems" he had. Some of the others did too. I always put in an extra carbon for myself. I made a collection of interesting items of similar nature and kept them in an envelope marked "Literature".

Some of the other Cadet Candidates got good specific jobs on the base too. Some became M.P.'s like Mack from New York. So there was quite a bit of talk going around that we would be assigned to the field so that we could get ratings. We were finally assigned. That was the first time in five months that I was "permanently" assigned.

Notices began to appear on the board, for anyone who could, to apply for aerial gunnery. I spoke to a few fellows that claimed that they had been drafted into aerial gunnery. But that was about a year later. Nash wanted to be an aerial gunner and decided to go for a plane ride. He got permission and climbed into a BT13 one night. The pilot knew it was Nash's first ride and flew only straight and level with a minimum of turns. After half an hour we began to wonder what had happened to the plane. After over an hour we identified the plane taxiing back to the ramp. A mighty sick Nash crawled out of that plane. He sat down at the edge of the ramp for a while and got permission to return to the barracks. He looked so pathetic that we didn't even have the heart to kid him about it. After that he never expressed any more interest in making like the birds.

One night there was a dance in town and we were invited. They supplied G.I. trucks. Mack hung up his gun and joined the fun. Course, he explained that he'd catch hell if any other M.P.'s saw him. But, surprisingly, it was a good dance. Otis was having a wonderful time, but then he was the best dancer there. Even I envied his smoothness. We never even suspected that there were so many girls in the vicinity just from walking around town looking for them. Course, no one was allowed to escort the girls farther than to the edge of the dance floor.

At 1:00 hours, Otis and Mack and I and the rest came back to our barracks to find that the other Cadet Candidates were all packed and ready to ship out early in the morning. We were supposed to leave at 5:00 hours. I tried to get to town early the next morning after finding out that we would not leave for a few hours. I did want to get my third such uniform from the cleaners. But early that morning I was told that there wasn't enough time before we shipped out—that evening. When we got to the station we found out what had happened to all the old obsolete decrepit railroad coaches. There they were, just waiting for us. We started to beat the dust off the seats. But we had to run outside to breathe while the dust settled back, at its leisure, not to be disturbed again. There were three fellows to four seats. The most comfortable place was on the floor and it was just as crowded as the layers of seats. Those who tried to keep their uniforms clean, used newspapers as insulation between themselves and the seats. But the smoke from the engine threw soot over everybody and everything anyway.

08/CADET PENNY ARCADE NASHVILLE, GA. SEP 1942

The train pulled past the city and then the word was passed around that we were going directly to Camp. Soon our hopes and expectations would be realized. We were to take the Cadet exams and become full fledged Cadets training to be flying officers in the Army of the United States. Everyone was thrilled and excited. We got off the train, fell into formation and proceeded up the street to enter our glorious Cadet Camp. We passed the gate and saw some real honest-to-goodness Cadets standing outside the barracks waiting to greet us. As soon as we came within earshot of them we started to yell Hello to them. But the greetings were almost instantly squashed when they loudly chorused: "You'll be sorry, you'll be sorry".

It seemed to be the password. Everywhere we turned they yelled it to us. At first we thought they just wanted to have some fun. But it wasn't more than a few days later that we joined in yelling it at some new groups that came in. And by that time we almost felt like we meant it.

When we got to Nashville all the non-coms started ripping off their stripes. Among the first to draw K.P. was the Tech Sgt. with us. Only the Corporals and Pfc's(Privates—First Class) got out of it. It was surprising how quickly we became an homogenous mass of privates. It was particularly amusing to see the privates who came around after the first meal wearing shirts from which stripes had obviously been torn.

We could hardly wait for our turn at the local penny arcade—Coney Island without the pennies, or nickels but lots of mechanical gadgets to test co-ordination. Well, a good part of it was not very amusing. Two solid days of writing answers. You've probably seen the kind—if the square is larger than the circle, blacken #1; if the triangle intersects the star, blacken #3: if it does not, cross out #4b. There were questions about history, arithmetic, algebra, machinery, current events and various and sundry other subjects. Each section of the exam was timed so that we all had to take the same amount of time for each part. So the fast ones who finished a little early had a chance to massage their fingers and work the circulation back up. Then we also had some large scale maps and small scale maps of the same areas. We had to match the sections of the large maps that the small maps represented, even though the small scale maps were turned every which way with reference to the large scale maps.

Then we took the physical TYPE 64 exam which accurately determined if our dogs had fleas or if we could stand on our right toe while lifting the left heel up to the back of our head, touch our left shoulder with our right hand and pat the top of our head with our left hand.

After which we were told to wander through the next section and amuse ourselves. They had one machine where you try to hold a spike inside a hole about a quarter-inch in diameter without making any physical-electrical contact with the sides of the hole. Said contact lights a bulb and rings a bell, but you don't get any cigars for that. The number of times the sides are contacted are to be counted by the participant. The instructor is supposed to talk excitedly all the time, telling the eager candidates how nervous they are, how much they will be embarrassed by washing out, that they no longer have a steady hand, anything else that comes to mind to promote additional contacts under simulated (or stimulated) pressure. The G.I. we had was, however, very cool and calm and only let his voice get excited. My impression, however, was that he was repeating his lines for the umpteenth time and appeared more bored than anything. The harangue was periodically interrupted to call off seven single digit numbers. After the machine is turned off the numbers had to be written in the correct order and the number of times that the bulb was lit. I counted something like thirty-five times, which seemed about average.

There was another machine where they tested depth perception by bringing two clothes pins on a looped-string next to each other about ten feet in front of you and controlled by the string in both of your hands. I lined them up once and was told to go on. I wondered why everyone else got three tries while I only got one. Later, I realized that I must have very good depth perception even though I wasn't aware of it before. We all got together after the "show" and took it all apart. As usual nobody knew the score so we all expressed more dislike than approval.

The brother of an old friend was supposed to be stationed nearby but there just didn't seem to be any time to look him up. We only spent a week at Nashville and most of the Cadet candidates didn't ever get to go to town. One of the guys went through the fence, across some fields and then on the road. He saw the town and came back. In climbing under the fence he ripped the seat of his pants. But since he didn't get caught he figured that it was well worth it.

Nobody knew when we were going to ship out from the Camp so I took one of my uniforms to be cleaned. Sure enough, the next day we received orders to ship out and again I couldn't get my uniform back. I didn't have a single khaki shirt or pair of pants left to my name. So to make up for it I drew an almost complete Cadet uniform outfit.

Just before we shipped out there was the usual physical exam. They asked who had sore throats and such. I raised my hand for the old cold I'd gotten at Monmouth. The other Cadets jumped on me and said that I'd never ship out. So that was the end of that.

09/HEY, MISTER SAN ANTONIO AVIATION CADET CENTER, TEXAS SEP 1942

Of course, now that we were officially CADETS we were to be addressed as MISTER in contrast to "SIR" for Officers and "SGT" or whatever for E.M. As we got near the city of San Antonio we seemed to come through the back door. We saw the dirty streets, forlorn houses sadly in need of repair and paint, unkempt little ragamuffins playing in the yards and alleys. We left the train and took trucks out to the field. We rode past one camp, then another, then up to a new one on a hill. They hadn't finished clearing all the land. The barracks were set up in neat orderly groups and covered a large area.

We were dumped out of the trucks in front of the headquarters and greeted rather unceremoniously by a Sgt. The first thing he did was ask us what we were. We immediately shouted with (what we thought) was pardonable pride and effervescent enthusiasm: "PILOT CADETS". Without batting an eyelash he said "Why, we expected 250 Bombardiers, I don't know what they'll do with you". Of course that made us feel good and glad and we all felt like joining in and giving him a great big hand—right across the face. We spent the next month attending lectures, drilling and doing KP and guard duty, taking PT etc. etc. Repeated the sex and morality lectures. We were very lucky if we got open-post on week ends. Open Post is like open house except in reverse—everyone goes away for a good time.

Here there were so many thousands and thousands of Cadets on the Air Corps fields around San Antonio, that supply items of any kind, were apparently a major problem. So some efficiency expert, that's what they were then called, decided that each Cadet was entitled to twelve (12) sheets of toilet tissue per day.

At one of the regular inspections the C.O. told me to get my hair cut. I had been hoping to get by until open post. I'd seen the other fellows return from the butcher—er barber shop. But getting a direct order like that was not to be trifled with. I found the barber shop appropriately located in the latrine area of the barracks. As soon as you were seated the barber waded through your hair leaving large wakes in their path. Whatever hair they missed in the 43&1/2 seconds could be kept. If you wanted a shampoo that added a dollar to the 35 cents and took an additional 15&1/2 seconds of time. It was shear accident if you still looked socially acceptable when you left.

I went back to the C.O.'s office and showed him my new hairdo. He burst out laughing. I told him that he had ordered me to get this haircut. We Cadets were supposed to take pride in our dress. Our grooming was always expected to reflect credit upon us and the service. Yet the barbers were perfectly free to ravage our appearance. He asked helplessly: "What do you want me to do?" I told him that I wanted him to register my complaint although I knew that nothing would come of it.

NICK - CAMP CROWDER

FT. MONMOUTH, N.J.

NICK - IN A SLING?

AT THE ALAMO, TX

10/CRAZY CADET CAPERS KELLY FIELD, TX NOV/DEC 1942

According to regulations, an Aviation Cadet was supposed to rank just below a West Point Cadet and above a Master Sergeant. But that condition only existed on paper. Among the Cadets themselves it was another story. The unusually fine extra-special system of HAZING was supposed to have come directly from WEST POINT. There a few notable men rebelled and were successful in abolishing the irritation of hazing. They were then classified as "Cadet Customs", but not affectionately. At first everyone felt rather silly going through the motions, then P.O.'d (pissed off) and then just tolerating the system because there wasn't much else to be done.

About then it was just about time to turn around and begin enforcing it on the newcomers. Then they introduced the sitting brace. That was a lulu. The regular or standing brace was bad enough. The Cadet was supposed to stand at a very rigid attention, even exaggerated, subject to the upper classmen's orders etc. But a sitting brace was another matter. Depending on the Cadet's size, the subject/victim placed himself two feet from the wall. Then bringing one's body, from the head to the seat, flush against the wall and stretching one's hands horizontally forward, palms facing each other, the desired position is attained. Desired by the upper classmen, of course. The idea is to form straight lines and sharp corners with the extremities forming a question mark (except for the head). It's just a sitting position without benefit of a seat. Everyone crumples before they pass out. I don't know of anyone who held the prescribed position for as long as two minutes. If you don't think it is hard, just try it. It wasn't long after that the customs of hazing were supposed to have been abolished. Then there were the fellows that had just returned from combat and weren't in any mood to do "toy soldiering".

About this time most of the prior service men had learned to stand at attention in the approved manner. A brace was just called a rigid attention but it had more oomph to it. There were cute little details—that they used to delight in yelling to the unfortunate, such as: PULL YOUR CHIN IN, THROW YOUR CHEST OUT, WIPE THAT SMILE OFF YOUR FACE, PUT IT IN YOUR POCKET, HOW OLD ARE YOU?, WELL LET'S SEE 19 WRINKLES IN YOUR NECK. SQUEEZE MY FINGER—at that, the upper classman placed his finger between the shoulder blades of the victim who then had to bring his shoulder blades that much closer together forcing the chest out that much more. REACH FOR THE GROUND—stretch one's hands as far down as possible. One fellow was told to do that in the changing of the guard review. He gave everyone a good laugh when he reached over forward to literally touch the ground. Even the inspecting officer had to laugh. At each and every command some improvement had to be shown or else: "Gigs will be given and tours will be walked".

MAKE A NASTY MOVEMENT-bumps. PULL YOUR STOMACH IN. Physically as well as theoretically it was impossible to talk in a regular brace; so as soon as the bracee talked the upper classmen claimed that answering was grounds for gigging.

Each time the stomach was pulled in, the Cadet's belt would have extra length not needed anymore. The upper classmen would then eliminate that theoretical extra length so that the belt kept getting shorter and shorter and stomachs were forced in more and more. In such cases the only lasting relief was to make sure that one didn't possibly "WASH BACK" and remain a lower classman for an additional four weeks. Although in such cases (which were extremely rare) the former classmates usually left the Cadet very much alone except for sympathy.

Then there was the sleeping brace. It was a real trick to do it. That one required that the Cadet stretch out horizontally with his arms as close to his feet as possible, chin in, chest out, stomach in, keeping the body six inches above the bed at all points. Luckily we left before they started enforcing that one.

Sloan had spent a number of years in South America working for some big company. He had a sizable pile of sugar and brought his own car to pre-flight. After he was in the Army, the Army wrote him requesting the use of some of his land. He said Yes, natch. When first exposed to hazing (note above) he was ready to quit. Then he suffered it, then liked it and by the time he became an upper classman he loved it enthusiastically.

Someone got the bright idea that we could only leave the barracks in pairs. Each time someone wanted to go anyplace, even to the P.X. across the street, he had to have company and it wasn't always convenient for even numbers to travel together. One evening, three Misters were caught outside. The U.P. (upper classmen) immediately put them in a brace and asked them what was the idea. One of the Cadets answered quickly: "He's our tail gunner, Sir". "Well, if he's your tail gunner, he's supposed to travel backwards and keep muttering: "Rat-tat-a-tat, rat-tat-a-tat". After that tail gunners/third persons, became popular.

Upper classmen took their positions first at the wall sides of the tables at meal times. The lower classmen took the remaining places near the center aisle. The latter entered the mess hall on the double (double-time marching/running). The one who drew the seat in the aisle was automatically the gunner and on his right and left pourers (for one or two pitchers of liquids as milk, water etc.). The gunner's job was to "buy" sufficient food for the table from the waiters. Lower classmen were required to keep their eyes on a point while eating, in front of them at eye-level, the distance immaterial. If an "upper-" caught a "lower-classman" with his eyes wandering he would ask: "Are you going to buy the place?" Once in a great while the lower classman would answer: "Yes".

For punishment, lower classmen had to eat square meals. They were then not permitted to look at their plate. They had to sit upright at attention. After getting food on the fork (or spoon) it was to be brought up vertically to the level of the mouth, then horizontally into the mouth. Such procedures could greatly decrease the quantity of food consumed.

The exercise and schedule whetted everyone's appetite. After about two weeks of P.T. (physical training) here though, I was finally completely rid of my cold. The schedule didn't allow very much time to eat. The serving plates were not filled enough to go once around and the upper classmen served themselves first. So some of the lower classmen had to depend on the efficiency and eagerness of the "gunners" and waiters in order to get enough food.

Sometimes, for excitement, there were auto races at the tables.

These were conducted in either or both directions around the table. One Cadet would start humming or buzzing at maximum volume and quickly sweep his head from one side to the other. The Cadet next to him at the end of the sweep would pass it on etc. and then wait to pick it up again the next time around. This would go on as long as it pleased the table Commandant.

There was another popular game called "Famous For". The head of the table would ask the lower classmen: "What are you famous for?" Mr. Saul had come up from serving in Panama—naturally in the regular Army. The winters in San Antonio were proving too much for him. He had requested release from the Cadets because he was freezing. The C.O. gave him special leave to go into town and buy some winter underwear. In spite of his tender age however, he proved himself able to handle Table Commander Rick. Some of his answers to: "What are you famous for?" were:

> "I'm famous for being the owner of an athletic bird that makes people jump, Sir."
> "And what sort of bird is that?"
> > "A goose, Sir."
> "I'm famous for cutting toilet seat in half, Sir."
> "And what is that for, Mister?"
> > "That's for half-assed Cadet Officers to sit on, Sir".

Lower classmen were confined for their first four weeks. Upper classmen got open post once a week. When I was a kid I could not understand why some of the Legion conventioneers at Chicago reunions would go on drunken sprees and acted so unrefined as to throw water filled "balloons" down on passersby from their hotel rooms. But by this time I was beginning to comprehend the desire to lose one's inhibitions and control.

Tex and I got pretty chummy and we liked to go to town together. One thing I admired about him; not just that he could drink and drink and not stagger or become pugnacious; but he never bragged about Texas as much as he liked it—especially in comparison with almost any other Texan. Incidentally, Tex and I bought a pair of regulation pilot's wings at the P.X. and didn't breath a word about it to anyone for fear of being kidded.

During one brace, Bruce blew smoke in my face. He was much smaller than I and had washed back into our class that week. I came out of the brace and told him that I would hit him if he did it again. He was called Bruce because he used to tell the barracks about his teacher and him. He was one of the big cutups at his school and one of his teachers took him in hand and indoctrinated him in sex. After that he was no trouble at school. But there was no excuse for his blowing smoke at me. Then I resumed the brace.

Once a week Cadets were required to change the bed clothing and we were issued two clean sheets and a pillow case. Every morning we had to make our beds so tightly that a quarter would bounce properly when thrown on the middle of the bed. If the sheets weren't taut you would get gigged. I would make my bed when I changed sheets and each night I would slide between the sheets and slide out again the next morning. I would then spend about fifteen seconds drawing the sheets tight. I never got gigged for my bed. But that was because of how soundly I slept and I'm sure most of the other Cadets were similarly worn out each night. I would spend about five minutes relaxing before getting into bed. Thirty or forty years later that might be called meditating, except I didn't try to think of anything.

Finally the great day approached and we looked forward with alternating exultation and apprehension. Moving into preflight was definitely a relief after wondering and wandering for so many months. The whole class was marched into a large area carrying barracks bags. When we were first inducted, part of the equipment consisted of two barracks bags. Then we wondered what the second one was for. This was six months later. Now we wondered if we could possibly carry a third bag when we were already staggering under two.

11/LOOK MA, I'M FLYING—OOPS VICTORY FIELD, VERNON, TEXAS NOV/DEC 1942

We pulled into Victory Field in the morning. The first thing was to register and get barracks. The second was to get our flying clothes. We had to try them on. That took care of the first day. They lined us up the second day according to height. Chopping us off by fives we were assigned to our instructors. We had to salute them every morning when reporting and address them only as "Sir".

Vernon was a nice little town. Once in a blue moon there arose some minor differences between the GI's and the natives. Life for the most part was serene and easy going. Natchurly open post had to be exciting and we all went to town even if we did no more than to say hello to the same faces we saw at Camp. The natives were friendly including the girls. There were only a few places to go in addition to our country club, but we all enjoyed the social life. On Christmas morning all those Cadets who were still in bed at the field, got breakfast served to them by the porters. The Gadgets then passed the hat and everyone was happy.

The ground school taught us theory of flight or why an airplane flies. We could discuss all the technical aspects with our teachers. The navigation in ground school taught us how to tell direction by the compass and what to look for to check our position. Then we learned how to read maps. We did not take any maps along for our regular flights. They always tried to have one or two cross-country flights in primary. These would be flying from one city to another and then return to the base. The first cross-country would take in cities that were all in sight of each other on a clear day. None-the-less it was invaluable practice. They taught us the differences between true, magnetic and compass directions which were variation and deviation.

They also taught Metro (Meteorology/Weather) in ground school. That's where Cadets get the ability to look at a date and tell w(h)e(a)ther? We had plenty of weather too. A white flag meant that students could solo. A yellow flag meant that the instructor had to be along. A red flag meant that the field was closed to all flying. We disliked the yellow flag most of all after we had soloed. A student was expected to solo in from eight to twelve hours.

The second biggest washout seemed to be in the first two to three hours. The biggest washout was right after soloing. After the fifteen hour check there was a sharp drop in washouts. With twenty hours under one's belt it was acknowledged that one could fly.

B.S. was my instructor. He was rumored to have washed out of Advanced Flying Training because of some physical defect. BS broke us in right. We alternated with the other half of the class to fly half a day and go to ground school the other half of the day. We could study on the flight line while waiting. But nothing else was allowed, not even horseplay. They had coke machines around and having nothing else to do, most of the fellows would drink a few cokes every day. Then there were those handshakers who insisted on buying cokes for their instructors. It was one of the standing arguments that cokes would or would not affect one's stomach at altitude. We were supposed to fly at 5000 ft. for most maneuvers. There were a choice few early ones that were permitted to fly at 500 feet.

The first ride was just to get acquainted with the atmosphere. The instructor took us up and told us to watch for a few points on the ground. All we did was fly straight and level. On the second trip we held the stick for a few precious seconds. We also did shallow and steep turns. That is, BS did them, I just happened to be along.

We also had to do "S" turns while taxiing. That was the only way we could see what was in front of us. The last step in checking before take-off was running up the engines and checking the magnetos. All airplanes have twin ignition as a safety feature. It is strictly against regulations to take off with a plane that loses more than one-hundred rpm when checking/switching the magnetos. The plane vibrates noticeably when the engines are revved up and this can create quite a dust storm on a dirt field. The standing joke in primary was about the green Cadet who blacked out while checking the mags.

Once BS told me to keep an eye on the field and then tried to make me lose it by doing acrobatics. I surprised him by pointing out the field immediately after he turned around. I had no problem becoming oriented to the air view. I also had a good sense of direction, which is normal.

Before a Cadet soloed he was called a dodo or kiwi bird. The kiwi is supposed to fly in ever-decreasing circles until both ends came together and then mutter: "Keeryst its dark in here". Whenever a Gadget pulled a Knucklehead the instructor would yell: "Isn't it dark down there?" or "Grab your ears and pull your head out".

We finally did get to practice take-offs and landings. We went over to the auxiliary field for such things. Made one take-off and landing. Then on the next landing we blew a tire. BS made me check that it was blown. Then he made a diagonal run of the whole auxiliary field which included two traffic patterns. At the very last moment he pulled the stick and flipped over the fence at the end of the field and we were off. With fingers, eyes and toes crossed. The flat tire didn't make any difference in flying characteristics. But without extreme care it could cause a ground loop while landing. A ground loop is where one wing tip runs circles around the other while the pilot watches and turns red and the instructor gets hot under the collar—unless the instructor did the ground loop. It had rained the few days previous and the whole field had not completely dried. In landing BS coolly picked out a large mud puddle and ever so gently placed the plane in it. We rolled less than 20 feet, stopped the engine and calmly walked away leaving the plane in the center of attention on the field. We did take another look to find that the rear tire was flat in addition to the left tire. BS was very much surprised that I didn't get at all excited. I had actually enjoyed it. But I think he still had the erroneous idea that I was only a hairs-breadth away from getting airsick.

We went out to the auxiliary field and made two circuits. I was mostly responsible for the second landing which wasn't very good. BS climbed out and said that it was all mine. I didn't feel anything in particular. I was wondering just what kind of a landing I was going to make. I lined up with the field and gunned the engine. It was a good takeoff but that wasn't hard. Like BS always used to say: "The big danger of flying was not up in the air, it was putting the plane back on the ground". I climbed to 500 feet and levelled off and made a turn to the right. The first time I came in for a landing I was going much too fast and thought I better try again. As I passed the center of the field I waved to BS to show him that I still had control of the situation and he shouldn't worry. He told the others about the hand wave but never mentioned it to me. The second time I came in for a landing I applied too much rudder for drift and immediately started drifting sideways down the field. I saw that I couldn't put it down without landing in the safety zone that ran the length of the field through the wind T and separated the two opposite traffic patterns. The third time I figured my landings were not going to get any better so I might just as well set it down anyway. Which I did. BS came up to me and told me to go around once more and make one good landing and then we would go home. I tried to obey orders but I just didn't. I was bringing the ship in too fast at eighty miles per hour and didn't know what to do about it. BS had shown me once but didn't explain it. I was very much afraid of emulating those fellows who had stalled out on the approach and damaged the plane. Again I tried and brought it in on the third time around. We went home then anyway.

Arriving back at the field BS reached over and removed the tape from my forehead. I had forgotten about it completely. Then those of the others that hadn't yet soloed crowded around and excitedly asked me how it was. I wasn't particularly elated but only felt that I had passed a step which by itself didn't mean so much. Just that I had taken a plane around the traffic pattern by myself. There was one fellow that went around about thirty times. We heard about it at the main field while he was still up in the air. He kept going around and around and around. They finally sent someone up to force him down. When he told us about it he very seriously explained that he just didn't like any of the first twenty-nine approaches and waited until he made one that he liked. He did have enough gas left to get back to the main field so that was that.

Most people have the idea that the first solo flight is the most thrilling experience to the fledgling flyer. Taking off and landing is something but it doesn't hold a candle to the first solo spin as far as I'm concerned. The first time I took a plane off the main field I was given instructions to practice what we'd been doing all along. I practiced faithfully all the maneuvers I'd been instructed in. First I did climbing turns, then a few gliding turns, then a stall and then a spin, well actually I decided to settle for another stall. There I was all alone at 5000 feet altitude and nothing between myself and the ground except the seat of the plane. I checked my safety belt again, cleared the area below me and calmly told myself that if I were to continue flying that it has to start now, with a spin. Otherwise I must just as well go down and tell them I didn't want to fly. That was all. There was no alternative. I suppose I was pretty scared. But I didn't consider it at all just a question of fear. It was a basic required maneuver of flying.

I did go into the spin on the second start. There was plenty of breathing space between the starts too. The plane stalled okay. Then I could feel my heartbeat stepping up its pace. The blood started pounding through my temples and I tried only to concentrate on the events to time my reactions with. The plane winged over slowly enough; but as the right wing went down it gathered speed like a rocket. I quickly plotted the wingline against the terrain below. The plane kept winding up faster. The momentum threw me towards the outside of the turn. As soon as I saw that we had made one and one-half turns I started the recovery. I kicked hard on the opposite(outside) rudder and waited. A moment later I was thrown to the opposite side and I pushed forward on the stick to avoid another stall. The plane went into an almost straight dive and then I pulled back cautiously on the stick to regain altitude. That is the point at which most people black out in primary. All the blood rushes to the seat of your pants. Your limbs and body feel like they have leaden weights attached and you can see all and do nothing. After the violent change in direction from down to up has subsided you apply throttle and climb back up to the desired altitude. Checking the area again I saw that I had done between two and a half and three turns that first time. Only about half a dozen spins later could I feel confident of applying the rudder and stick correctly to limit the turns to two and no more. Some of the rides in Riverview or Coney Island are more violent than any correct maneuver in primary. But the park rides NEVER approach the velocity of "plane" ordinary maneuvers.

There were a lot of things that were illegal in primary. But that sometimes lent an air of enchantment to them. After most of the fellows had soloed and we all had about twelve to fifteen hours Tex began to get ideas. He wanted me to follow him. That was one of the biggest regrets of mine in primary. I wanted to get through so badly that I would not usually think of risking it by getting caught goofing off. Tex came back from the flight line one day and said that he had done some loops and boy was it fun. I told him that if he would do snap-rolls as he bragged, then I would do loops. We got planes and checked each other's numbers. We took off one after the other and met over the Red River Valley. It was really fun flying formation—about a half mile apart.

He did some snap rolls or what looked like snap rolls so I started on a loop. I dove the plane to 120 miles per hour airspeed and pulled back firmly on the stick. It was a rather tight loop. When I got to the top, on my back, the engine cut out. I could feel that the plane wasn't stalling so I kept on going. As the nose came down the engine caught again and I was immeasurably relieved. I had already started picking out emergency landing places and wondered what BS would say. I lost track of Tex and forgot his plane number. We didn't get together like that again.

 I felt real good that I had done a complete loop before we had been given any instruction or authorization for it. Although Tex was doing snap rolls by then, that didn't dampen my elation. Most of the fellows were just going along. Tex didn't seem to care too much if he washed out. He had a good instructor though.

 Dennis, who was the smallest Cadet on the field took up a plane for a solo mission. A piston blew out on him. Someone saw him make an emergency landing. Then the rumors began to fly thick and fast. Before he got back to the field he had: "Parachuted, been lost, burned up with his plane, walked back from his wreck, was coming back in an ambulance, seriously hurt, not even scratched" and anything else that anyone could think of and repeat. He came back to the field in a few hours and immediately went up again with his instructor for a ride. Then they took him to the dispensary for a complete physical checkup. He wound up with a band-aid on his forehead. He had made a cross-wind landing and used a couple of trees to stop on a short emergency field. He was quite the hero for a while. The plane wasn't damaged too badly.

 Felix's mother came out to visit him. She was shown around in the best style and had a very enjoyable time with her son.

Taking the train back in the afternoon she was very thrilled. Apparently one of his classmates had flown alongside of the train for a few miles. It was a sight that she would remember for a long time. She was certainly glad that she could be sure that he would not do any dangerous flying like that. Felix had flown that afternoon after his mother left the field. He told us that he had spotted the train and flown alongside for some time and then waved to his mother. How could he then tell her?

One of the guys said that a Cadet from a former class had been washed out under special circumstances. This Gadget made a practice of landing in his girls pasture. He then took the girl up and taught her to solo in eight hours. His instructor happened to be going out with the girl too. Something slipped, possibly the girl, bragging to the instructor and the Gadget washed.

One morning Ladd came into the barracks and gathered up our flight and excitedly announced that there was a fellow at the gate that had four new tires for sale (this was when you needed a coupon etc. to authorize a legal tire purchase during the war). Ladd said that BS thought it would make a nice gift for our flight to buy for him. I immediately felt that this would be the same as bribing him and in no uncertain terms said that I would not be a party to such a deal. That kind of killed it because none of the others would then speak up for it. Ladd then had the precious job of breaking the news to BS.

About two weeks before BS left, he knew he was leaving. So he had each of us mark up as dual time, from two to six hours total that he sat on the ground. We didn't like it but we knew better than to complain. Every instructor on the field would have been against us. It was the old case of the good ones not desiring to make waves, to take action against things they didn't approve of. I was very grateful to the instructor that informed our new instructor, a Mr. Mason, who was probably the best instructor on the field, that we had a half-dozen hours of solo time marked up as dual. I prayed that he would stay. I learned more in the total of forty-five minutes that I flew with him than I had learned in more than double that time with anyone else. But he was joining the Navy. That was the start of the end. Even on our local radio station they announced that we were becoming notorious as having washed out more instructors than any other flight. So the remaining four of us were split up. Niles went to one, Ladd went to another and Otis and I went to Klinker. He was taking his first class through. He had just washed out one Cadet and was relieved of a Student Officer who had ear trouble. Everyone said that Klinker had really tried to get that Cadet through so I thought it was a break for me. But to this day, I don't know for sure. Otis went on an emergency leave and was far enough behind in hours so that he could gracefully be washed back.

    I got a ride with Klinker. He whispered the whole trip. I could hardly tell when he was talking and when he wasn't. He seemed to mumble all the time. I listened as attentively as I could because I figured that instruction was what I needed. When we finished the first flight together he told me to remember everything that I had been told. I hadn't even heard a third of what he had said. I didn't even know enough to speak up then.

    I got my thirty hour check at thirty four hours. Lt. Valor gave me an Army check ride first. I gave him everything I had and figured I had good reason to think that I had passed. Twenty minutes later I had a civilian check ride. I was sure it was illegal to have two check rides in the same day. But again I said nothing. I was just too tired to give a damn because the Army check ride was much more important. The civilian check rider wrote a rejection slip and the skids were greased. The next day I was taken for another check ride by Klinker who wouldn't dream of saying yes when the checker said no. I didn't give him a very good ride that time either.

When one of the Student Officers told me that Klinker wanted to see me it didn't take much imagination as to the reason. He informed me that for the three rides that we had together, he had turned in three rejection/pink slips. Which meant an elimination ride. I figured that I still had a 50/50 chance of coming through. I asked him that if I passed, then could I still have him for an instructor. He, of course, said yes. He then talked to the check rider and I would have given a pretty penny to know just what he said. I was so bored/tired with the civilian check that I amused myself by immediately snapping my head in the direction of the field after every single maneuver. The civilian check rider probably thought that I wasn't properly oriented. I didn't particularly care. The civilian check wasn't final. When it was over I listened very attentively to his criticisms which I thought were basically very good, with the exception of that orientation and roughness. He said that I was rough on the controls too. They closed the field ten minutes after we landed because of rough air but that didn't count at all.

The next day I got the same Army check rider, Lt. Valor. He asked me if I had run into trouble and I said yes. I gave him just about as good a ride as I had three days previously. But there was a major difference—I was on an elimination check ride now. I did a number of maneuvers just as I would have done with BS. Lt. Valor wrote them down as not being according to the book.

But that was the way that I had been taught them. He asked me if I were trying to show him if I were an HP (hot pilot). I told him that the last thing I wanted to do was to show off on that ride. I asked him how I came out. He said that I was through. I asked if that meant finished and he said yes. So I saluted, dropped my chin on my chest and walked off the field. The next Cadet in line for a check ride checked the plane for flight. To say that I was down-hearted is to put it most mildly. It was closing a very important chapter of my life. Like cutting off a living part of my being. In spite of the aggravation I had felt at not learning the way I wished, I had tremendously enjoyed flying. There was a thrill to it that would be hard to replace. If you have piloted you should know what I mean. The others cannot appreciate it. The individual mastery of the rules of flight can thrill you to the core of your existence.

 The folks back home are told. If you do or don't write home and tell them, the CO of the field writes home a very pretty letter saying that for the safety of the student he has been eliminated and needs comforting and encouragement. He just isn't the flying type and must be gently reconciled to it. He doesn't possess the necessary qualifications etc. and etc. I wrote a letter home and listed all the complaints that they reported on the last check ride and also the reasons for my objections and said to save it for future use. I was PO'd (pissed off) but good.

 All the fellows crowded around when they heard and about half of them expressed their sympathy at my elimination. That was a real consolation. It was more of a surprise to them than myself. They all wanted to know how it had happened. I told them, in case it might do them some good. Even the Officers and Cadets in my flight were surprised. I told Mack that yesterday Pilot training was the most important thing in my life but that today it was no longer. He said that was taking it like a man. Yes, that was taking it. I wasn't going to complain. I'm still kicking myself for not complaining—but there's no proof that complaining would have done any good.

When the Board met they tried to explain why I was eliminated. What burned me up additionally was that when the reasons were listed I was told that they were in technical language and I therefore couldn't be expected to understand them (although I did). They didn't seem to think that they were supposed to have given me sufficient instruction to understand them. I was asked if there were any questions. I didn't have any questions, I had some complaints. But again I kept still. I didn't find out until later that some Cadets had complained and been reinstated. I just asked about meteorology and engineering. They said that those fields were closed and that as long as I had gotten a perfect mark in the Navigation test I would be sent back as a Navigator-Bombardier. Which is what happened. The biggest reason I didn't ask to be sent to the GI Army, although it sill seems silly, was that I didn't care to give up the Cadet shortcoat. When I considered the many more months ahead of me I felt like a professional Cadet. "What did you do in the war, Daddy?" "Oh, I was a Cadet".

Washing out is supposed to have come from England. Referring to the plane returning from a mission. At the end of the flight the pilot would tell the E.M. to wash out the dead gunner (or bombardier, navigator, pilot or?).

12/SECOND TIME AROUND SAN ANTONIO, TEXAS FEB/MAR 1943

Here I was inducted into the E.P. (Eliminated Pilots) Club. The initiation consisted of removing the top half of the propeller from the Air Corps pin. That was to distinguish us from those who hadn't been around. Now Cadet Wood, who grew up in the same neighborhood as I, was coming through for the first time. When I told him that this was my second time around, I could see the change in his expression. He looked at me as if I were a poor relation, as if I had failed to do my job. Not feeling very guilty, I was amused at his attitude and was willing to let him meet some more E.P.'s so that he might better understand the situation. I did not think it at all worthwhile to explain anything.

The Reclassification Board called me in for a routine interview. The Board consisted of one Lieutenant. He asked me questions about my washing out. I told him that it wouldn't get us anyplace. But he still wanted to know. So I let him have it—what I should have said in Primary. I wasn't taught properly. The record should have been: "Lack of Instruction" instead of "Lack of progress". It had been said that I couldn't keep a second coat of paint on my car. Mentioning this as an indication of how good my coordination was; well, I hadn't been taught to fly like that. Yes, I could fly. But I was going through the motions monkeyfashion, just a copy-cat. In time I would have learned myself. As for instance I didn't know what reference points were and how they were used in climbing turns until long after we had covered climbing turns.

Five minutes after we started he said: "This isn't getting us anywhere. If I ever hear that you've talked to any of the Cadets here you'll get G.D.O. (Ground Duty Only)." To which I neither said yes or no. I didn't tell the new Cadets anything I thought might hinder them. But the other E.P.'s used to discuss their washouts.

Our particular squadron, #110 was pretty good to Eliminated Pilots. The Cadet Colonel was an E.P. and took the whole squadron staff from the E. P.'s. As a result he got good cooperation and the C.O. was very well satisfied. The Cadet Colonel and the rest of his staff all got Open Post once a week.

Shortly after I got in the CC checked the barracks and decided that yours truly should to be doing something. Got on guard roster and KP once and didn't like it. So, I started at the bottom of the staff ladder. I became a runner—one of the messenger boys hanging around the orderly room. I was then at the opposite end of the staff from the CC. I got Open Post with all the rest of the staff. That in itself was good. Soon after that, as head runner, I practically had the run of the place. We were exempt from practically all other duties. No more KP and guard duty. We didn't drill or take PT. It just wasn't convenient. For the inspections we arranged to be elsewhere if we worked it out right.

It was generally agreed that pull made a lot of difference. Yates was a surprise to us though. His dad was a General in the Medical Corps. Yates had gone AWOL in pre-flight for a few days. Upon returning he got right back into the swing of things and nothing was said. But in BASIC, he encountered some difficulty and washed out. Now he was classified as alternate G.2 (Intelligence).

13/MORE OF THE SAME ELLINGTON FIELD, HOUSTON, TEXAS MAR/JUN 1943

When we entered Ellington Field we were dumped off in front of the main P.X.(Post Exchange). No one knew what we were supposed to do. After a little persuading a few of the Cadets walked into the P.X. with me. I figured that if we weren't allowed to use this P.X. this would be the only chance to go in and plead ignorance. It took but a few minutes for our group to swarm in and swamp the salesgirls. At first they were reluctant to sell us anything because they must have had direct orders from Major Baits. But they got into the swing of things before Major Baits showed up and shooed us out. It turned out that this P.X. was reserved for Officers alone.

We were then all assembled in the theatre and given a welcome speech. The first words were: "Do any of you recognize me?" The speaker was none other than Major Baits, a well known Hollywood character who parlayed a speech impediment, that he didn't have, into a big career. And I do mean character. When he told us of the Sunday tea dances he stated specifically that the boys could take the girls home and he didn't care what happened after that. He paused for applause so obviously that one could easily feel the general antagonism run through the theatre. He may have helped some of the fellows at some time or other but no one ever even heard a rumor to that effect, let alone any proof.

Because of the predominance of EP's no one would have stood for any hazing. Anyway, it was the policy of the Navigation School not to have hazing. I was in the last bunch of EP's to repeat pre-flight. Otherwise I would have gone straight to Advanced Navigation.

As far as the ground school went, I was so P.O.'d that I didn't care to expend much effort. But then it wasn't really necessary. The school duplicated pilot pre-flight almost to a "T". Brian and Carl also applied themselves. Brian came from New Orleans. His dad was a wholesale grocer and got a government contract once. Some red tape made him reopen and make a very slight change in his packages. Feeling the government was to blame he never took another government contract. Brian was very religious too. He'd missed going to church only one Sunday in his life. What a record? I too wanted to know what had happened that Sunday so he told us he was on a boy scout camping trip and there was no church within walking distance.

Carl was from Texas and was almost enjoying his social life in the Army. When his home-town girl-friend, Wanda promised to come down he positively glowed at the thought. So for days we would tease him incessantly and sing: "I Wanda Who's Kissing Her Now", till she showed up.

Our flight seemed to enjoy singing more than the others. We had a pretty large repertoire that we kept adding to as we went along. We even changed parts of Alouette when someone got into trouble. That was the story of a Gadget getting into trouble on open post and getting to walk tours. One week end it poured for forty hours and forty minutes on and off. On Saturday morning the field was soaked. No one in an authoritative position could be found to cancel the S.M.I.(Saturday Morning

Inspection) march. As the time approached the feeling of bitterness increased. When the bugle blew it was still raining and we fell out in our GI rainstrainers. Ordinarily we were permitted to sing until we got within one block of the reviewing stand. But by that time we had all tacitly agreed that we certainly weren't going to stop singing for any such group of C.S.(chicken-style/fowl) Officers. The band was playing the Air Corps song. Only one Lt. had come to the judges stand. As we marched by we practically screamed the words to the song at the top of our lungs. So what happened? That was the only time that we ever won the Marching Contest.

Eric slept in town without getting permission. He already had a stock of gigs to walk off by then. So he joined the band as a bugler and was appointed a Cadet Lt. Since Cadet Officers were not required to walk tours he had all his gigs cancelled.

One character skipped the train and went AWOL. He stopped off en route to pick up his dad who then drove him into Camp. No cries, no complaints. Oh yes, his dad was a General. This Fritz told the fellows, when he became a FULL FLEDGED FLIGHT LEADER, that he really wasn't supposed to fraternize with the rest of the flight but that he would be a regular fellow. He was very much incensed when one of the fellows told him to: "BLOW IT OUT" and didn't pay any attention to his commands to cease. He must have expected to graduate as an extra-special, higher-ranking, fuller-fledged Lieutenant.

Burns, my older brother, also in the Air Corps, came to visit me and said that he would ship me his folding iron when he went overseas, which was supposed to be imminent. He had been to Ellington Field before with the Air Corps. As a ground person he had helped build the field before his Group moved elsewhere. We went to one of the dances in town that night. After he sent the iron one of the fellows asked to use it. A little later the thought occurred to me that just maybe the fellow didn't know how to use an iron. But by the time I reached the other end of the barracks the iron had imprinted its image in brown on the khaki slacks.

BERNS & NICK 1943
ELLINGTON FIELD. TEXAS

14/AERIAL GUNNERY HARLINGEN, TEXAS JUN/JUL 1943

"AERIAL GUNNERY", (with John Garfield) from the moving picture of the same name. It was easy to see where the pictures had been taken. We called the gate that had the long avenue lined with palms, the HOLLYWOOD ENTRANCE. I dragged out the old 8mm movie camera and took pictures too. They even came out all right. We then ran a sequence on an introduction to the exclusive E.P.(Eliminated Pilots) club. It looked pretty silly. Shon and I did the motions while Eric took the pictures. But there wasn't any rehearsing. We couldn't spend time rehearsing and gathering an unappreciative audience. They wouldn't understand.

The town wasn't far. We walked it a few times. There was a nice swimming pool, some bowling alleys, taverns, etc. The post had a nice beer garden and the WAC's (Women's Air Corps) were very sociable with Gadgets. One of the guys met a former model in the WAC's and was getting very interested. There wasn't all that much inducement to go into town. All two girls in town were very busy. Well maybe there were more than two girls in town. But you wouldn't think so if you ever tried to get a date.

Silver (Silence is Silver) came with us to Aerial Gunnery. Hadn't changed a bit though, still as obnoxious as ever. Everyone as usual, was exposed to PT. It was rather on the rough side here.

There weren't that many that goofed off but most of those that did were very careful not to be obvious. Silver had his name taken for goofing off on one of the exercises. He turned right around and took the instructor's name. That made the instructor stop and take notice. He inquired into certain circumstances. The next thing we knew, the First Sgt. was coming around looking for five references, to confer upon Silver, a Section 8 (mental disability) discharge. Right after that, upon the least excuse, the characters in the group would go around saying: "Hey, do you want to get out, I can get you four other signatures. Won't cost you a cent either".

Geek also accompanied us to gunnery. With him around, there was never a dull moment. I'm not saying that it was good or bad. It just wasn't dull. We took our instructions in little groups. Five of us had an exceptionally good instructor. We practically coasted through the course on what he had taught us the first week. We started with BB guns, then 22's, then shotguns. First, at still targets; then at moving targets. The trap shooting was loads of fun. The bird-houses have machines that throw clay pigeons about sixty feet. The object is to pepper the bird so that it powders. Any good hit makes the clay bird disintegrate.

The shotguns are quite deadly at close range. With a choke the range as well as the kickback are increased. They stress safety very emphatically on the range. There's too much potential danger to become careless. The cardinal rule is to never point a gun at anyone unless you intend to shoot them. We were even told that some of the instructors would rather have a good marksman point a gun at them rather than a beginner because the good marksman might be outguessed. But it's anybody's guess where the beginner is going to send his bullets.

On the ground range everyone messed together and I do mean messed. There was no segregation. We not only ate with EM and Negroes but we also ate with the Officers in a big long barn/mess hall. One night some baked ham spoiled due to not being refrigerated properly. Half the Camp came down with mild cases of ptomaine poisoning. They felt bad in the barracks in the early evening after eating the spoiled food for breakfast. The ambulances were kept busy all evening and into the night while some of the cases walked over. The dispensary was filled and surrounded with stretched out groaning figures. We left a few days later and heard that some very drastic changes were subsequently made. After that we thought twice before criticizing any food going into the garbage cans.

Dan and Ward and I were sitting at one of the long tables (they were all the same length) when a Negro sat down. He quietly ate and departed. Dan of course, being a Southerner, had been brought up to feel that Negroes must be kept in their place in the South. I am not apologizing for him, merely explaining. To mention that otherwise he was a swell fellow is superfluous. He just couldn't see Negroes. When this one had gone Ward turned to Dan and asked: "Well, does your food taste any different?" Dan hit the ceiling then and for a while I thought I was going to be a referee. But Dan didn't strike poor little Ward although the latter's remarks had certainly struck a raw nerve.

When we got on the trap range everyone was being extremely careful, upon threat of elimination, among other things. It was also excusable to slug anyone who got careless with a gun in his hands. As usual, Deek was trying to bolster up his courage by impressing everyone with his ability when handling his deer rifle (in civilian life). We were inclined to believe the sincerity of his tone until he missed consistently. The others were mixing up their misses with some hits. The previously experienced trap shooters weren't doing too much better than the beginners so we felt that was pretty good for us beginners. But Deek still missed with clock-like regularity. So the half-dozen of us that were on the same bird-house with him started to kid him about that dear deer rifle of his. He said that shotguns were very different. When he started to answer our jibes, he naturally turned around to face us. Doing so with the gun in a waist firing position. We knew he didn't intend to shoot us. He just didn't realize that the gun was pointed toward us and it probably had live shells in it. None of us said anything after that. We did not josh Deek anymore that period, we waited until we got off the range. We all agreed that our comparatively little pleasure couldn't measure up alongside the ease with which he might have an accident. On him, accidents seemed natural. When we got to the skeet range, he did have one. Skeet is just shooting the bird (clay pigeon) from different positions. The last steps are shooting two birds in succession. They are propelled from the bird house at the same time from opposite sides of the range. The closest bird is shot and then the second one which should still be in the air. Once in a while, the first burst gets both birds, particularly when shooting a little late. That's no good, it says so in the rule book. Well, on one of these quick-firing jobs, Deek didn't put the gun up to his shoulder right and the kick expended itself on his physiognomy. Being expressed in a neat (?) black eye. After that he was very gun shy.

When we got to firing the machine guns they gave us actual practice with first, second and third position stoppages (malfunctions), wrong head-space and of course the runaway gun.

Thereafter when something went wrong with anything from an eversharp to a jeep someone would yell: "Second position stoppage" or some such silly saying. Whereas before, a handshake was so called, he now had his head space too tight. The runaway gun merely brought out the old familiar invectives as the first operator in the class usually let go of the hot gun. That was a real NO, NO.

There were a few real close ones. The firing required almost instantaneous reflex and reaction. The pressure of fast accurate timing is felt most when learning. The bird houses always got their cues from the student doing the firing. But Shon didn't step out of the way quick enough once and Emil fired before he realized that Shon was still there. The muzzle of the gun released its shot about two inches from Shon's face. Shon laughed and said that if it never came closer he wouldn't have anything to worry about. It didn't but he did. Emil was still visibly nervous after they got back to the barracks. I met up with him a year later and he seemed to have recovered from the incident. Course he had other things to worry about then. A good many months later I heard that Shon got killed in California while completing his flying training.

Accidents can happen even while being careful. The last step on the ground firing was to go around an oval track on the back of a truck, still using shotguns to hit the birds ejected from twenty five bird houses along the route. On one of these trips, after I had my turn, I was standing directly in back of the Cadet that was firing. The other spare student and the instructor were in the other two corners. It was probably the 13th birdhouse that throws the bird straight to the truck. The Cadet fired but about a third of the bird still remained intact. Upon impact of the shot, it was thrown off its straight course and no longer kept going up. Instead it curved around the shooter right for me. As soon as I saw it I started to duck but I got hit right between the eyes. Blood flowed quickly for a few seconds. Then its slowed to a trickle. When we dismounted everyone wanted to know what happened. I was slightly embarrassed at getting in the way. A band-aid over the bridge of the nose pretty much covered everything up.

From the Caliber 30 we graduated to the Cal. 50. We took trucks on the ground range in small groups to the various ranges. The guns were braced by steel pipe mounts set in concrete about four or five feet apart. While one man fired the Cal. 50 another one held the metal link belt holding the rounds. The object was to fire very short bursts for accuracy. But firing short machine gun bursts takes a quick trigger finger and practice. I fed first, standing between two guns. The target men scampered to safety, the red flag went up and the instructor yelled fire. Fire? like hell, I was so surprised I don't know how I stayed on my feet. We'd been told to wear cotton in our ears and I did. But the thunderous crash almost split my eardrums and I couldn't tell which way was up, let alone how the belt was going. I was lucky to be holding the belt loosely so I didn't follow it into the feedway. By the second round I got used to the thunderclaps and shaking concrete. In fact when I shot I hit the target with 50% of the bullets—at 25 yards. That was probably the best shooting I did on the ground range. I guess that was a little above average. After all, as long as I'm the one that's guessing I might as well be good.

After a while on trap and skeet shooting we used trap turrets. The trap houses were built up on platforms about forty feet high. Thus we could shoot in a special top turret. A guide stood on the side of the turret checking loading and firing for the operator. We worked in teams of two for loading and firing. When they wanted volunteers to load everyone was reluctant. Finally, so that we wouldn't be held up any longer, I stepped forward on the basis that Fred would help me. I figured that he had the best coordination of the group. I had seen him on the basketball court and was impressed when he didn't seem to rush but always had his hand out for the ball just in time. I loaded while he tripped the bird release. He got his cue from the guide on the turret. I just placed the bird on the machine. We stayed there till all the other teams had shot and emptied a few boxes doing it. That way we wouldn't have to climb all those steps again. It is my considered and deliberated opinion that we fed birds faster than any other team and we felt we had done ourselves proud.

We went from the turrets with shotguns to platforms on trucks with shotguns. These trucks, four or five at a time, went around an oval road along which were twenty-five bird houses. These bird houses would each be tended by a Cadet. That Cadet would watch through a window and when the trucks passed a certain spot on the road, would release the bird (no relation to the Bronx cheer). We would alternately ride and tend houses as usual.

After we got back from the ground range we were again in the same instruction groups. Then something happened that made the guys happy—especially Flaherty. "Deek" was washed out on the basis of his ground firing record. Everyone felt much safer. In fact, Greg felt like celebrating, he'd been in the same plane with him and that he felt was an unwarranted and unwanted danger. After word got around, we were really surprised. We couldn't find even a poor rumor of a similar washout happening before on that field.

As we got into the AT-6's for air firing, I noticed one of the other pilots in the flight. I was positive that he had been an upperclassman at pre-flight and primary. I tried to catch his eye before we took off but didn't succeed. I tried in the air and I was sure that I caught his eye because shortly after that we started a rat-race to the gulf. That's follow the leader in the air. They tried to turn the planes inside out. A few days later one of the other guys fell out of the plane. Since his safety belt was attached the pilot pushed the plane down faster than gravity. That way the fellow got on top of the plane and just climbed back in. I enjoyed that first ride since primary so much that I didn't waste any time aiming. We got into position with the target sleeve and I let go a dozen bursts in quick succession and winged over out of the way for the next Cadet. I did that for the second hundred rounds too. So the pilot and I had a good time together.

About the fifth time up I drew the same pilot as twice previously. So I figured I wouldn't waste any time. The previous time when I'd had a short round and signalled the pilot that I could fix it, he nodded and waited. That day the first time we got into position, I waited for him to signal and then I pulled the trigger once. That took care of the first hundred rounds. I didn't feel that was quite the right way to practice though. The next time we got into position I pulled the trigger two times to fire the second hundred. I got my highest score that day.

The next day, after I had emptied my guns one of the other Cadets followed his pilot's wing-waving signal and started shooting before they were in position. I didn't know what had happened till later. They said that everybody scattered all over the sky. On another mission Dale fired three bullets at the target sleeve and one of them severed the wire holding the sleeve. So that mission didn't count. No target sleeve to count hits, no marks. It had to be scheduled all over again—except for the three bullets. We each got two hundred rounds per day for six days. Ten percent hits got the Marksman's Medal, fifteen percent hits got the Sharpshooter's Medal and twenty percent hits got the Expert's Medal. I got two hits under fifteen percent. The day they awarded the medals for air firing in AT-6's I wrote home and said they just handed out medals so I got in line to get one, which, it seemed to me to be just about the same effort to earn one.

The last trip from the ground range was a splash party. That was fun. The object was to fly about fifty feet off the ground and shoot at sticks set up in the water along the shore of the gulf. There was no score kept. Some of the fellows just dumped their bullets intact over the sides. It required firing out the side of the plane between the wing and the tail. They told us that wings had been shot off that way so that we should be careful. But we were good guys. We just emptied the guns at the sticks as quickly as could and then formed a sort of Lufberry circle. That's where one guy puts his nose on the other's tail. We flew this circle above a house on a sand bar, which appeared to have a lot of boy scouts in it. At any rate we started diving on the house, then climbing up and revving the engines. Over a dozen kids then came running out of the house to cheer and wave. That was fun.

Of course, if our barracks were dirty, as they usually were, the top sgt. passed the word on to us very emphatically. As usual, one of the things we were threatened with was no open post. But because they didn't have much experience with the way the Army treated Aviation Cadets, we were treated just like E.M. which we liked fine.

That part of the Rio Grande valley was supposed to be the most fertile in the States. Incidentally it was farther south than any other place in the States. We were only about 25 miles from Brownsville and the border. The plant growth reminded me of the jungle (even though I had never seen the jungle except in pictures). But there were more bugs and insects living in our barracks than any other place I've ever been in the States and the walls and floors were dirtier that any others we ever scrubbed.

There were various posters extolling the beauty of Mexico. And others saying: "You haven't seen Mexico until you've seen Rosita". We all made arrangements to see Mexico. We had to get passes and the fellows had to have their money changed into coins and two-dollar bills. It seems that some energetic enterpriser competed with our Government in printing and tried out all the denominations except two dollar bills. The Mexicans were therefore not satisfied with denominations other than two-dollar bills. Quite a number of the guys saw Rosita. She borrowed some half-dollars to do some tricks with eggs. What kind of tricks did she do? Well, I didn't see them; I guess you would have to see Rosita to find out. But some of the guys couldn't eat eggs for a couple of days after that.

Someone in charge at the base made a big hullabaloo about the sentimental value of a yearbook that was going to be printed. It was to be quite massive and impressive and we would surely want one as the years went by so that we could look back and remember the happy exciting times we had at Aerial Gunnery School with all our friends. Practically everyone ordered a copy at $4.50 each (1943 dollars). After all, it was sanctioned by the

Army. It's entirely possible that the volume was printed, published and packed for posting. I just know that it was paid for and not permitted any privilege of perusal. I just never got a copy nor do I know of anyone else who did. But such is life: "Give and Learn".

15/HOLD THAT HURRICANE ELLINGTON FIELD, HOUSTON, TEXAS JUL/AUG 1943

A lot of the fellows had made arrangements to get furloughs because of the time they had been in the Army. Practically everyone with a year and a half got a furlough through regular channels. Then there were those who got them through emergency measures with the okay of the Red Cross. The first week we were back at Ellington, quite a number got emergency furloughs. That was okay because we didn't know when we would ship out. The second week I got an emergency telegram. But they saw fit to question it. So I immediately put in for a furlough through regular Army channels while waiting for verification from the Red Cross. The Cpl. in the orderly room helped me fill out the request. Where it said date returned to active duty he said I should put down when I expected to return from furlough. The date should have been the day I was inducted into the Army. That difference may have been why Major Baits denied the regular furlough.

Though I didn't stop with that. I followed it through four different authorities until I got to the person who had stopped it. The EM who arranged Major Baits' interviews asked me if I had gone to gunnery school. I told him yes. Whereupon he told me to go back to the barracks and put my gunner's wings on. He seemed to know what the score was so I complied. I reported in my best military manner to Major Baits and threw him a Sunday highball. He returned it and asked me my business. I showed him the furlough request and told him that it had been refused. He said that he had done it and that was that. He really started to give me the business about how much he was working his fingers to the bone for all the Gadgets and all they did was try to pick bones with him. He almost had himself convinced.

The more he told me, the more I believed the rumors about him. He was a well known name in Hollywood. I asked him if I stepped out of the Cadets back into the Regular GI Army, could I then get a furlough. He immediately took that as an insult to Officers.

Saying that he would see to it personally that I didn't get a furlough by such steps. Then calling in a typist he asked her to write out my resignation. At that moment he was called out of the room. The girl asked me if I were going to resign saying that I should not. I just told her that if I were to resign from the Cadets I wouldn't give Major Baits the satisfaction of having contributed to it.

So we both waited for Major Baits to come back. Then I told him that I had come there asking him for help. If he couldn't give me any then there was no further point in continuing the discussion. He said that he would be only too glad to help but under the circumstances it could not be done. If I were a good soldier I would say: "Thank you, Sir", salute and leave. I asked him if that was all (if the interview was over)? Upon the affirmative I SILENTLY saluted, turned on my heel and left.

Some days later there was news of a hurricane coming directly towards us. There was a lot of talk of evacuating the planes to San Antonio and that the Pilots were all waiting. But then it became impractical to do that. So the planes were left on the field when the hurricane struck. Since I was waiting for confirmation to the emergency telegram I didn't go out when they told the other fellows to help hold the planes down. Some of the guys really had a tough time. By morning of the second day it was a problem just to get to the mess hall. A number of the guys had tried it and gotten blown off their feet. Two others and myself linked hands and did a duck-waddle all the three blocks to the mess hall. When we got there it was almost deserted. I asked the Captain in charge for permission to take some bread and jam back to the fellows in the barracks. He most regretfully informed us that it was against regulations.

The next day the papers came out with a big headline that the hospital was full of injured soldiers as a result of the hurricane and how much damage it had done at our field, at Houston and at Galveston. They also had a big spread about Major Baits putting on fatigue clothes and working diligently with the other soldiers to keep the damage at a minimum. I guess he had helped hold down the planes at the same place that the reporters were. Not one of the other soldiers I talked to saw hide nor hair of him the day of the hurricane. We were all sent on open post the next weekend and told that it was because we had helped so well in holding down the planes. A minority of the planes needed widely varied repair work done but most of them came through in good shape.

We weren't at all sorry to leave. The whole gang had missed most of the CS(chicken stuff). But that was more as a result of our unwritten agreement than anything else. We had all pretty much agreed to keep out of everyone's way and sight. So it was all hunky-dory. As long as we got open post with the rest of the field and sack sores the rest of the time.

16/ADVANCED NAVIGATION HONDO AAB, TEXAS AUG/JAN 1944

Getting a leave to Chicago I went to visit our younger sister's new apartment on the near north side. So I took the I.C. train from the south side and the Elevated and got off at the nearest station which was still a few blocks from her place. I walked in the approximate direction and figured that I ought to ask just to make sure. Just then a cabbie drove up and discharged a passenger and I stepped over by Stratford. The cabbie turned to me as another fare climbed in and said in a very impersonal voice: "Sorry buddy, I've already got a fare". I started to turn away when the passenger said in a very friendly voice: "Hop in—we'll take you there". Well, it didn't make too much difference. But being in a hurry and sure it was close, I got in. Then both of them explained where I was going as we drove the two blocks there. As I got out I asked the cabbie: "How much do I owe?" The passenger said: "That's okay, I'll take care of it" and continued in a very gracious voice and gesture: "You're in Chicago, now". How could I have the heart to tell him that I was a native Chicagoan.

My first mission was a flop. I added backwards wrong. We add backwards when we start with the Magnetic Course given on the compass. Then we figure out what our true course or track is with relation to the ground. Just a little technicality. My second mission was practically perfect. Lt. Schlub called me in and said that: "You could not possibly be that good at this early stage of the game." So he was only going to give me a 90 instead of 100. I thought that was more amusing than anything else. The next mission I again had trouble adding backwards. It continued until the ninth mission. I then got all my logs and checked each one for the addition.

On the first few missions I had taken my log to the barracks and spent about four hours fixing it to look good. I got a good mark but I didn't think it was worth the extra effort. So I never did any more barracks navigation. In fact by the time I got half a dozen mission in I wouldn't even bother to touch pencil to paper until seated in the plane. That is, with the exception of data that we had to take down during briefing (metro, weather, turning points, destination and any particular problem). I guess I was just too lazy. I worked all the time in the air and was kept pretty busy too. But once we lined up with the runway, my work was finished. I just handed it in as it was.

While standing in formation one day outside the Navitrainer Lt. Schlub was in charge of marching us back to our classroom. He had driven there in his new Ford Convertible and asked the flight who could drive. I raised my hand and he told me to step forward. But just before he handed me the keys he repeated point-blank: "Can you drive?" I thought that was so funny that I immediately burst out laughing. He handed me the keys when my laughter subsided and said no more except where to meet him. I got in and the first thing I did was to kill the engine. But I raced it a little after that and didn't have any difficulty. I didn't realize then how fussy he really was about his car.

In class, when Lt. Emil asked him to use the car for an hour Lt. Schlub asked Lt. Emil: "Can you drive?" Lt. Emil jokingly replied: "I just took two lessons last week". But the joke was completely lost on Lt. Schlub. He didn't want to turn over his keys until Lt. Emil reassured him. Lt. Emil got red in the face after noticing Lt. Schlub's reluctance. Another time Lt. Frank jumped on the running board just as Lt. Schlub was starting up. Lt. Frank got the door open as Lt. Schlub put on the brakes. The door swung wide and must have touched the fender. Lt. Schlub then stopped the engine while he got out to examine the extent of the damage to the paint. After that I wasn't so eager to drive his car. But he never offered his keys to any of the other students. I really couldn't fault him for trying to take care of his car. If you get the idea that Lt. Schlub was not popular, I would not deny it.

I changed instructors quite frequently. Lt. Schlub didn't want any students if he could get anyone else to have them. And he gave the orders for the Flight. We didn't seem to hit it off too well. The first time we met in the barracks he asked me what I was doing there. I said: "Waiting for Class 43-18. You're going to be my instructor". He replied a little testily: "Oh, no, I'm not". Well, he couldn't have been too happy to find that he really was my flight leader. Then the rest of class 43-18 came in. Hart said that if he had any idea that combat navigation was going to be as much work as the training he would quit immediately. He just wasn't that much of a hero. John and I double dated a number of times. He went on one mission doing dead reckoning. That is just a method using rate times time equals distance. John was lead navigator on the return trip. He was going along in great style telling the pilot when to turn and how much. He had his nose buried in his computations for some time. He then came up for air long enough to hand the pilot a 3 degree correction to the right. The pilot in the meantime had approached the field, entered the traffic pattern and was easing back on the stick preparatory to setting the ship down on the runway. But he took John's paper which showed a slight turn to the right. John, of course, had not realized that they were already there. The pilot turned to John and said: "I think this is the right runway".

Kean was going all out in Navigation ground school. He had the highest average in his class. But it was another story on the air work. He just could not put two and two together when his feet got off the ground. He didn't really get airsick although that's what they called it. His mind just seemed to refuse to function in a plane. Yet his classroom work was beyond criticism. Kean just couldn't bear to write home and tell them. Yes, that may be a good part of what kept the Army together more than anything else. The fact that any soldier's actions automatically reflected on his family back home.

While standing in formation as usual Bret spouted off. So I told him to keep a better rein on his tongue. He didn't think he should. As soon as the formation was dismissed he started swinging. He acted so wild that I thought there was nothing there. The others separated us quickly. To get caught red-handed would have been automatic elimination for both of us. Bret suggested following up the altercation. Now everyone knows that fighting only settles who is stronger. Silly, isn't it? But basically, being from Chicago and knowing that backing out of a fight is even more likely to result in a beating, I asked him to say when and where. We met outside the barracks where Bret started crowding me but I told him to be patient.

We squared off. Boy, was I going to teach him a lesson. And I sure learned one. Since it was so silly and because I wasn't yet into it, I was letting myself wide open. At first, he was practically hitting me at will. I didn't feel that hurt till after a little while I took stock and realized that my guard was rusty and wide open. Did I say WIDE OPEN? When his left came in my right was way out of line doing absolutely no good. He had a ring on his hand and was cutting my nose up very badly, Then it started to swell. When I touched my nose and saw the blood on my hand I really made some changes. I completely stopped Bret from getting through my guard so that he was basically through hitting me. And I was practically hitting him at will. But I didn't mark his face up. Then he offered to take his ring off. We stopped while he took his ring off. Then he dropped it. He insisted on finding it before we continued the fight. So both of us hunted and I found it for him. But Bret was tired of the fight and more than eager to call it quits. He offered to continue it the next day but by then it would be all over the post. I put some mercurochrome on my nose which made it even a brighter red. Then I put on a big piece of adhesive plaster which covered up the nose. But the doctor ordered me to remove it to help healing. I had the two biggest black eyes I ever saw. My pupils are naturally brown. Quite a number of the guys asked me how the other fellow looked and I told them truthfully that he didn't have a mark on him.

 The next day we were both called into the front office. Lt. Emil and another Officer questioned the two of us. They asked if we had been fighting. I was standing next to Bret but I didn't hear him say yes or no. I laughed and asked if they thought Bret could make me look this bad. The Officers laughed then and gave us a lecture on helping to win the war and not starting our own etc., etc. Later at night school the Lt. told me to ask Bret a question. The whole class roared. I did—and he answered. Then

I took it upon myself to ask him another question, which he became too confused to answer. I joined the class in laughing then. After that almost everyone suggested that we shake hands and make up. But I wouldn't. I still did not know why he had wanted to fight me.

As a result of my adding backwards wrong and changing instructors I was always getting check rides. Right after this the weather got bad and no one was flying. So everyone got behind. Thus there was no chance of my catching up to the rest of the class when the bad weather broke (changed for the better). The grades had to be in too soon. So it was decided that I would wash back.

Of course, I wasn't at all bashful when it came time to explain anything to the other members of the class. After all I had been an after-school teacher for advanced algebra. I even went up to the platform to draw diagrams for the class. However, I wouldn't go so far as to say that the instructors always approved. Getting the point across may have been like putting salt on an open cut. A number of times I gave advice to the fellows sitting around me. Dale sat directly in front of me. He turned around quite often to confer with me. At least it was quite often the first couple of weeks. After we had gotten a few tests back and his average was consistently higher than mine he thought better than to refer items to me. I didn't care. I then talked with him as little as the rest of the fellows. He didn't seem to have much social inclinations at all. Later, when the class finished and Dale was tagged for an instructorship, the rest of the guys moaned.

Squadron Three had been permitted to sit down at evening meals as they marched in. Squadron One had not. So I told Squadron One, when no Officers were around, that they also could sit down as long as they did it smoothly. Squadron One had been in the habit of wearing blouses to retreat formations. Then they would run the three blocks to the theatre to beat the movie starting time. That wasn't changed. But one evening, an eager O.D.(Officer of the Day) called the variation to my attention. I said the men had always been permitted to do so. When he complained of the non-uniformity of appearance I said that it would no longer be noticeable.

Then I announced that I didn't ever want to see a blouse in the front rank of the retreat formation again.

By showing the guys that I was a good buffer for the Officers I got a lot of cooperation. When I once gave the command for retreat at the end of the song as "Present Arms" instead of "Order Arms" they executed the latter. About a minute later when I realized what I had said I asked the guys about it. They laughingly confirmed the fact. I appreciated that cooperation. Another time we were lined up for the mess hall and I gave: "Column of two's from the left, forward march". Then the person leading the fourth rank properly followed up with an excessively loud "Forward March" for the next two ranks. I went over and told him that we didn't do it that way here and the Officers wouldn't like it. He was bigger than I and belligerent. "Well, that's the right way and that's how we did it in the Pacific". He looked like he was ready to fight too. I didn't particularly care. I very evenly and calmly told him that we still didn't do things that way here. Two days later he came up to me and put his arm around me and apologized for blowing his top. I told him to forget it. But I was surprised and very much pleased that he should think enough of Squadron goodwill to do that.

When we were studying sun time, star time, regular time etc. I made a diagram listing and explaining each kind of time and its relationships. All the students wanted a duplicate but only a few took the trouble to copy it. Lt. Floyd was interested and said that he would see if he couldn't get the school press to include it in the instruction material. When he volunteered for combat and I washed back, I gave it to my new instructor. He thought it was pretty good too. Captain Buck briefed us on our graduation hop. Telling us that the War Department wouldn't allow him to go to combat he used this means to pretend. Then, very carefully, he went over almost every detail of the route and things we might expect. He was a big gun in the school. I figured that here was the guy that could really push the TIME TABLE that I had laboriously constructed. I very optimistically showed it to him. He hardly glanced at it while I talked. His objections were immediate. Then he went on to explain how the school material was so good and how he had personally set it up. I could see it was a lost cause then.

Then there was the fellow that took two shots to make a fix at night. He worked about half an hour figuring out the information from the shots and plotted his course. He made two mistakes. One for each star. His LOP's (Lines of Position) were way off. Except at one point. That was the point at which they intersected. So his resultant fix was correct. The instructor was so surprised and pleased at such accurate shooting in the first place that he idly ran over the figuring. It was only then that the two compensating mistakes came to light. It was so unusual that the instructor told about it to everyone who would listen.

Such things were what might be called honest mistakes. There was also the fellow who got a check ride. The check riders came from Randolph Field so we called those trips: Randolph Rough Riders' Check Rides. They weren't supposed to count at all. It was theoretically a check on the instructors and not the students. Certain things were required. A celestial fix (stars), a pilotage fix(rate x time = distance), a radio fix(radio wave bearings), a ground speed by the sun, etc. One Cadet Group Commander was working like mad to no effect and the checkers were breathing hot on his neck. So he looked out the window, recognized San Antonio (he was from Texas) and noted it for the time. Taking two stars, he started shooting. Then figuring at what altitude (inclination/angle) he would have to shoot them, he worked all the way backwards until he got the information that would check through showing that he had shot a fix on that town. Theoretically not knowing what the town was below. He did not leave the field when the class graduated. They made an instructor out of him.

When I washed back to 44-1-1 I kept the rank of Cadet Captain and was made a Squadron Commander. Karl was a real F.U. (Fouler Upper). He got the bright idea that nobody in our flight should volunteer as Cadet Officers. I warned him that he was sure to be chosen anyway. He became leader of the first flight in the squadron. When Karl first started counting cadence for the squadron he was so slow that the fellows had difficulty balancing on one foot so long. I stepped it up a little but it was still difficult to get the rest of the flights together.

Then I hurried it up and started taking the count from the head of the column which was over a block away. Everytime I stopped and started again the middle and end of the column would have to change their step. Until one of the Cadets complained: "My right foot is the same size as my left foot". That was good for a laugh on me. I then realized that because of the distances between the front and center and rear of the column everyone did not hear the same "left" at the same exact time (it took so long for the count (sound/voice) to travel to the ends. After that I kept up a loud even cadence that I took from my own steps and tried to stay between 110 and 120 steps per minute. We all marched fine then.

In 43-18, the only really good instructors were the few that I had not had. With 44-1 I told the guys that something was wrong. I had gotten the best, repeat, the best instructor in the flight.

As we approached our last three weeks the instructors told us that we could vote for our own Cadet Officers. But we didn't. The list was called for before we had got to vote. The instructors put their heads together and I was left out. I didn't like it when they told the class who was what. Imagine my surprise when we fell out for mass formation two days later and one of the Cadets grabbed my hand and congratulated me. My name was third on the list of Cadet Officers. I was a Wing Ding. I would review the troops with the Cadet Colonel.

But that wasn't really so much. We picked up our Sam Brown belts at supply and wore them to classes. The next day Lt. Schlub came over to my desk at the far end of the room and asked me what my position was. I tried hard not to gloat as I told him. I knew before that he had nothing to do with my appointment.

I had purchased Lt.'s bars and had to return them later. I left the barracks with a Warrant Officer emblem on my cap per T.O. to attend the graduation ceremony. Everybody else in the whole theatre was undoubtedly more excited and thrilled as they went through the ceremony and gave out the wings. As usual there were several E.M.'s waiting outside the theatre. Upon throwing the new Officers their first highball(salute) they collected a dollar. I got halfway back to the barracks before I was saluted and it took the last of my folding money. We were paid right after that and checked off the field.

The last thing to do before leaving the field was to go to the Officers' Club and get some cokes. There was considerable curiosity to see what it was like. It was very nicely furnished and there was a circular bar piled with bottles, each having an Officer's name on them.

The first thing in town was to meet the girlfriend. Second was to rent a car and bring my bags to the hotel room when the flight was to have its party. Since it was so early we went for a ride and then took in a show. We didn't get back till very late and the party was over. Well, we had missed the party but I'd had a wonderful time anyway. Early the next morning I was on the train for home. It only took about five times as long as the last time by flying.

17/WHAT ELSE IS NEW? WESTOVER FIELD, MASS JAN/FEB 1944

Everyone reported to Westover Field in dire need of a rest. With the possible exception of those who had stayed with their wives. Don and I took the same train down. I didn't get Pullman figuring that I had been on so many troop movements without it that I should be used to sitting up. So I regretted it.

We looked over the town before reporting at the field. The first night we all went to a friendly informal party to get into the spirit of hospitality. Those were fine towns in the neighborhood. Everyone that wanted a date could pretty much get one. We had to be on the field at least a few hours every day. They were very strict about reporting to the theatre on time in the morning. There we learned what our schedule was. Some of the fellows liked the town so well that they decided they couldn't be bothered with morning schedules. They were immediately threatened with not shipping out on schedule if they did not mend their ways. And the Officer in Charge was perfectly serious.

We had to be processed for the umpteenth time. Don and I dated a couple of girls from the college and we went to one of the local entertainment spots. The girls had to be in early. I had about six shots—whiskey of course. Certainly no more. I usually didn't take that many. But the girls were going strong and I didn't particularly feel the effects at the time. The next morning, if not bright, at least early, we took a physical flying examination—type 64. I felt extremely sluggish. When the WAC (Womens Army Corp) stuck a needle in my arm for blood I had a premonition that it would take some time and told her so. It did take about three times as long as usual for enough blood to drain to satisfy the regular demand.

Right after that we had our blood pressure taken. My normal blood pressure is about 122. Passing for this test was 102. I tested 92. I told them that I felt sluggish at the time and that I was perfectly all right otherwise. Another fellow took it and told me to come back after I was all through with the rest of the exam. About an hour later the second fellow took it again and marked it down as 102. A passing mark. This was not at all worrisome.

Barney and I and a few others decided that as long as New York City was so close we might as well visit it. As Officers we no longer needed paper passes. We had off from Saturday afternoon to Monday morning. And took it. So six of us went to the Officers' Service Club at the Commodore Hotel. Barney and I went to a Hunter College sorority dance and met some very nice girls.

We didn't spend very much time on the field. But there were certain things that had to be done. One was to get assigned to a crew. That was done easily enough. They just assigned the men on paper. Only some of the men objected to flying on paper. That was when we found out that we were to fly in B-24's—commonly known as the Flying Boxcar. Then there was the Captain who was at the field a couple of days before he found out that he was being assigned to a B-24 for combat duty. That got him pretty hot and he raised the roof and burned up the wires.

By the time everything had cooled off he was going someplace else much more to his pleasure. Then there was the brand new 2nd Lt that stood up in the theatre one morning. He asked the ground Captain in charge: "You've got me, Mark, listed as First Pilot on Crew 62". "That's right", the Captain agreed. "Well", said the 2nd Lt his voice crescendoing: "I've never even been in a B-24". He apparently had come across some other pretty unusual things in the Army because he did not seem too confident of having anything done.

After making out my last will and testament and power of attorney the next question was where to keep them. It was merely a routine precautionary measure to be filled and sent home and hopefully not looked at again.

As per usual, we got shots (hypo this time) for everything that we couldn't provide notarized documentary proof of. Then I was paired with Bombardier Lt. Herb for crew #22 and a couple hundred of us took the train to catch up with the rest of our crew. We got Pullman. One of the fellows brought his wife so we had to be on our best behavior. We were shipped in civilian coaches so it took us only the regular time to get to Charleston, W. Va.

18/OUR NEW CREW CHARLESTON AAB, WEST VIRGINIA MAR/APR 1944

The morning after we arrived we met the rest of the crew. The first mission we went on together was just checking out to get acquainted. Here was the first time I really had to use the interphone. At navigation school all conversation was supposed to be over the interphone. But we either talked directly or used signs or passed notes. In other words we let the interphone pretty much alone. But now that I had to use it, my inexperience came to light. Everytime I picked up the mike I yelled, but good and loud. It wasn't long before they kept telling me either to whisper into the mike or else use it only for listening. They said I didn't need a mike to talk in flight. They didn't know anyone else that could make themselves understood in a B-24 during takeoff. After a half dozen missions I started to get into the habit of using the mike like a telephone.

That first mission our pilot, Paul, an ex-pilot instructor, was still checking the co-pilot, Peter out, an ex-tower operator. So we just leisurely flew up and down the coastline around Charleston. I'd brought all my maps along and was just using pilotage to keep track of our position. There was only 4/10's coverage (clouds covered 40% of the sky looking up or the ground looking down). After we'd been out a few hours Paul asked where Charleston was. I answered North readily enough. So we turned North and

Paul asked me to point out Charleston. When we came abreast of the mouth of A river I pointed out the town below. But it looked awfully small for Charleston. Paul questioned my information and said that he was going to get a QDR(Quadrant by Radio). Well, I got a little excited. After all, this was really the first opportunity I'd had to show what I knew. The last thing our instructors had drilled into us was to make our crews believe that we knew how to navigate whether it was true or not. Paul flew due east to get over the ocean. Immediately I got very busy getting a radio fix. In a couple of minutes I called Paul back and told him that the town in question was SBL (Savanna Beach) and how far we were from Charleston and what our heading should be now. He just took it in and agreed. But it served as fresh kibitzing material for the crew for weeks. I'd never seen Charleston from the air before but that was no excuse.

 I only missed a few or four trips during the couple of months that we were at Charleston, but the fellows kidded me about goofing off so much. Besides, it seemed that every time I didn't come along something happened. Once when Paul came in over the field when there was a ground fog right on the runway. He had been complaining a little about his eyes but we never paid any attention to that. We still considered him the best pilot on the field. He had more hours in the air than a good many of the instructors there. But he was still very respectful of the instructors. On that particular mission he made a good approach and set the plane down ever so gently on the fog bank. Then it plopped down a few more feet to the ground. He was embarrassed to say the least. The fellows sure needled him about that. I learned about it the next morning. Another time they had a gunnery mission. The gunnery instructor had been on a drunk the night before.

Rather than risk being punished for not meeting the flight line in good condition he flew. He didn't use much oxygen either. Before he or any of the others realized it he was out, but good. After that he stayed on oxygen all the time till the end of the flight.

Here was where we first got into the habit—from the time we reported to operations for flying until the very moment that we started down the runway everyone hoped that if something was going to go wrong it would go wrong right now. If anything questionable developed it was followed through to make damn sure that it would function properly. Otherwise we wouldn't have to take off. But once the throttle was advanced and the engines were revved up we automatically changed and prayed that nothing would go wrong. Particularly did this happen when the crew had the required flying maneuvers for the course finished. We would have to fly anyway because every field got as much training time as possible.

Another day that I didn't fly the navigators were coming back with stories of ground speeds of five miles per hour. It turned out that there was a wind aloft at 20,000 feet of 115 mph velocity. The bomb run was directly upwind. The true air speed was 120 mph so the airplanes were going only 5 mph in relation to the ground. None of the planes crossed the target that day. One of them did stay on the bomb run for over an hour before giving up.

One of the things we noticed about all our instructors was the preponderance of B-17 men. We knew at that time that there were more B-17's in use earlier but I can't say that we liked that. Later there were more B-24's than any other plane including B-17's.

About a half-dozen missions later we went up on a night radio trip. I got busy in the nose shortly after takeoff. A while later the navigator instructor joined me. He glanced over my work and then concentrated on getting a good radio fix. He was not that small and getting around him to the work table was a project. Work table? If you rested both hands on the table you covered it up. I was just eager enough to make a good impression figuring that a plane can only stay up for so long and one might just as well keep busy as not. After about three hours the instructor moved away from the radio dial and announced that the radio didn't work. He hadn't gotten a single good fix. However, he said he would turn in a good report. It was an enlightening trip nonetheless. The instructor took his sweet time about getting things done and his nonchalance (savoir faire) was impressive. After that there was a more conscious effort to work more slowly with a greater economy of motion. This was one of the first airmen to return from combat—him being the Navigator from the Memphis Belle. The third and last phase of our training was concentrated on the bombardier.

One of the requirements for the navigators was a 1000 mile over-water trip. Each plane took a short crew and a long crew. The short crew consisted of the Pilot, Bombardier and Engineer. The long crew omitted the co-pilot and some gunners but included the engineer and radio operator. Paul was chosen for the long crew and we were paired with Lt. Todd. We were briefed to fly by radio and dead reckoning on about three dog-legs to Cuba. We were to fly to Jacksonville, then cross over to the Southwest tip of Florida to just outside of Havana, all in formation. With all the material and information in the nose, Barney was eager to get some pilotage time (visual navigation) so he took the maps and I got busy with D.R., figuring out the course computations and then checking with the actual course. There was quite a difference. We were still flying in the right general direction. It wasn't very difficult to follow the course of the plane but that course was certainly not what we had been briefed on. After about three hours of flying when we were over the flat terrain of Florida, the idea of the lead plane became obvious. The lead plane was going from city to city and thereby changing course about every fifty miles. When flying in formation its very hard for the pilot to hold a heading long enough for the navigator to get an exact drift reading. So I didn't have a very good wind to base my figuring on as we drew out of sight of the mainland of Florida. But the weather was fine and we flew over Key West and then sighted Cuba still holding our place in the formation.

We joined the others on the ground and were assigned completely screened in barracks. We heard that they had some conscientious objectors working on the field and that their wives were permitted to take civilian jobs here. It was amazing to find the camp so spic and span. It was without question the cleanest and neatest camp we had been in to date. But there was a good reason for it. Any carelessness in sanitation would have shown up immediately in the health of the personnel. It wasn't a naturally healthy atmosphere. The cities weren't too clean but there wasn't much room for improvement at the camp. The waiters in the Officers' Mess were very neat and courteous. But we were most amused. In spite of the long time that the waiters served Americans, the Americans had to speak Spanish to make themselves understood. Usually its the other way around. But if we wanted milk we had to ask for la leche or not get milk. Those of us who had taken Spanish then tried to outdo each other remembering all five or six words that we knew. But after a few days a little more came back to us.

We were warned that the island was full of foreign spies, intrigue and what have you. There were supposed to be a number of taverns etc., on the island where they had pictures of Hitler and gave the Nazi salute with every drink. Anyone witnessing such things was not to become too excited. We were not only warned against talking too much we were impressed with the effect of our actions in town being judged as the whole American Army and not just us. The permanent personnel officer who briefed us for our trip into town did a rather thorough job. And he was very emphatic on that point. His blood pressure rose visibly as he spoke. It was apparent that this was a particularly sore point with him. The Cubans were not inviting the American personnel into their homes. They had no opportunity to meet the better class, and why? Simply because when the airport had visitors and did allow them into town, they did not conduct themselves as gentlemen. As witness the officer that got himself so drunk that he stumbled into the most exclusive and elite hotel in town and urinated in the lobby, with loads of witnesses present. At this point the Officer's voice broke with emotion but he kept on telling us that we should return to the field before we make such spectacles of ourselves as that. We were the first bunch allowed into town since that incident and if we did not conduct ourselves properly the next bunch would not be permitted to visit Havana.

Next, he warned us not to whistle at the upper class girls lest we find ourselves with a duel on our hands. If we didn't get beat up first. They did not consider a whistle a compliment. But there were plenty of girls that would give us what we wished for a price. Also that price might include the worst venereal diseases of India, Africa and all points east and west. This was veritably a mecca of the world and each part brought its own particular brand of venereal disease, usually not as yet typed and classified. The island was used to world visitors and catered to all. They drew no color or creed lines—only mazuma was the password. Also, the silk that was offered us was strictly pre-war as none had been imported for years. The alligator bags were not too good at the time. But certain other items rationed in the States could be advantageously purchased here. As film, for instance; if we could get the right size. They did tell us that all the cabs operated in cahoots with the joints and the houses. Going from one to another joint until the fares had been run dry.

But we were all eager to see the town. It was like a holiday. We waved to all the people and laughingly pointed out the children running around in their birthday clothes. It was fun.

In Havana I paired up with Barney. He wasn't looking for girls either. I wasn't even looking for a drink. I did want to get some souvenirs and see what the town was like generally. During our walk we were approached by a dark southern gentlemen who inquired if we were interested in some nice eighteen year olds. He even offered to drive us over but we graciously declined.

Late in the afternoon and early in the evening the trucks gathered to take us back to the base. A few of the fellows had such a good time that it was an effort for them to walk to the truck. A few rode up in cabs while a few others waited and took cabs out to the field to race with the curfew. While we waited for the trucks to fill up the street peddlers gathered with their nick-knack wares and tried to push them at bargain prices. What cost fifty cents at twelve o'clock could be had for twenty cents at five o'clock.

Which didn't make the twelve o'clock purchasers feel good. I had bought some of the castanets but insisted that they inscribe Havana and Cuba on them. When the price came down that made a difference so I didn't feel too bad. We made the arduous trip back to camp after dusk had fallen. Most of us were happy but tired from the visit and didn't give much thought to singing or comfort. I figured that the briefing officer had given the fellows a good talking to and had really made an impression so that the guys wouldn't go chasing after women in town. But my impression sure was disabused on the ride back to the base.

The return trip briefing consisted mostly of telling the pilots that their navigators were not to be allowed to use the radio. We were to fly from Cuba to the Bahamas and then fly by the sun to Charleston using only sun shots and dead reckoning. I didn't have any charts for the ocean so I had to use a blank mercator (world map on rectangles). We were given the latitude and longitude of the three points involved from other maps. We got the metro info and then were rushed for takeoff. Todd and his bombardier and engineer flew back with us. I gave a course to the Bahamas and a few minutes later was notified that it was a collision course—should the pilot go to the right or to the left. I said right because I wanted to cross the Bahama field in making the left turn to Charleston and not cut short. That way I'd get the time of departure from the Bahamas exactly. I was busy all the time on the first leg figuring out the information for the second leg and just recording the information for that first leg. About 4/5 of the way there I took stock of our track and then called Paul and gave him a thirty degree left turn to our first destination. I found out later that Cole told Paul that he would never take a thirty degree correction from any navigator. But Paul said that navigation was my department and he trusted me. We split the first destination and turned to go north by west to Charleston. Adler told his pilot to fly about 315 degrees. He'd overheard one of the other navigators and mistook the heading of about 350 for 315. He saw land long before any of us only it turned out to be Florida.

When Don got airborne he called his pilot on the intercom and frankly told him: "I'm the navigator, you're the pilot, we both want to get there so I'm going to use the radio". That was all there was to it.

I called Paul and told him to put the plane on auto-pilot and I would shoot the sun. As he did I took a two-minute shot and then two one-minute shots. Getting a difference in speeds of about ten miles per hour. After finishing the computations about 45 minutes later I told Paul to fly manually and took two two-minute shots. I repeated the latter and with all the computations got a ground speed between 171 and 172 mph for all but the first set. That looked very close to reality and I started looking for our destination as there wasn't time enough to complete another set of shots.

Leaving the Bahama Islands there was nothing to do but check wind and heading for the first hour. Shooting the sun would only give ground speed and not course and it would not serve any purpose to get a ground speed for twenty-five to fifty miles. So I set up the astro-compass and checked the heading of the plane. According to the astro-compass calculations there was a difference of about seven degrees. But I didn't feel that was correct. I checked with the pilot's compass and then decided to rely on that. The drift over water was very hard to read without a gyroscopic driftmeter so that was only estimated. Figuring as close as practical between the drift and astro-compass readings looked like we would be no farther than Charleston field or thirty miles to the right (east). With a good ground speed the ETA (Estimated Time of Arrival) would be good either for the field or a turn to the left of the thirty miles or less. So there would be no possibility of getting lost or not knowing what to do and when. Getting out the map of Charleston and figuring backward gave an estimated time of crossing the coastline. It felt pretty good when that came out within a minute's margin. But most surprising was to find that our course brought us right over the airfield. While expecting the ETA to be close, fifteen seconds was really closer than expected.

Paul found out that only a couple of others had split destination similarly. Within a mile and a minute. So he thought that was wonderful. I laughed and said that celestial navigation wasn't really that accurate. Later I was amazed that my system of shooting followed to a "T" the system that the Army brought out to us about two months later. Not wanting to brag or be too modest nothing more was said. Figuring that whether the crew knew or not, how accurate or inaccurate our position was, wouldn't change the facts, the crew was not advised of my confidence or lack thereof.

19/RADAR AND WAIT LANGLEY FIELD, VA APR/MAY 1944

When we got to the Sea Search Unit we naturally assumed that we would be assigned to sub-patrol duty. Instead we got quite a change of plans.

First we found out that we were there just to wait for a new bombardier radar operator and a radar ship. Also, while we were waiting we would go to various ground schools and we would fly radar operators on practice missions. On some crews they had taken the bombardiers and on others they had taken the navigators for radar training. Meanwhile Barney was enjoying a thirty day or so leave before reporting to Florida for instruction. The bombardiers had found out that they would not start school for over a month and had sent a telegram to Washington requesting leaves. And they got them wholesale. Some bigwig at Langley Field decided to give idle navigators radar instruction so we were taken out of ground school classes and attended a little gray schoolhouse by ourselves. There were a number of GI's there that really understood radar. We had an Officer for an instructor. Although he did an excellent job only a couple of others and myself could claim to understand what he taught. It was only a difference of a little technical radio background.

Then the second of my two front teeth went bad, thanks to Bret. The dentist examined the tooth when I returned to have it pulled. The gum was bleeding a little when I left but not too badly. Returning two days later because the bleeding had not stopped and then had gotten much too bad for comfort. The Doc put some stuff in my mouth and the bleeding stopped and I left. The next day the bleeding was as bad as ever. I implored the Doc to do something about it that would keep. He said: "It is nothing at all serious, so you are just losing some blood". To which I answered: "Yes, but I hate to see so much good blood go to waste". Then I got the first of a number of bridges to cover the gap of the two missing front teeth.

One particular afternoon when there was nothing going on, word came rushing through the camp from the flight line that all planes were grounded. There was no evidence of a storm brewing and we were all puzzled and curious. Everyone was wondering what was cooking. Then someone found out that a group of unidentified planes were flying over Norfolk Bay. All flying crews were alerted but we still did not know what was going on. The alert had passed from mouth to mouth and not through any official announcement till the whole field was aroused. There was quite a letdown when we found out that a group of BT-13's were on a cross-country hop and had flown way off course. The radar sets had picked them up and because they were not cleared for that route had sent out the alarm.

As long as we were not training for anything in particular the whole crew tried to get a regular leave of absence from the field. We ran around trying and failing to get get a regular leave. So we checked operations to make sure that we were not going to be scheduled for the next few days. Then we left. As long as Paul would stay on the field he could keep track of the schedules for us. We took the boat across the bay and then the railroad. The next day Peter stopped off in New Jersey and I continued on to New York. With about forty bucks to my name that was considered to be enough. Each day a call was made to Peter after Peter had called Paul to find out if everything was still okay.

New York is a fine town. The tempo is supposed to be so fast that even native New Yorkers are afraid to go to sleep for fear they will miss something. Times Square is still the only outdoor place in the world I have been where there is always somebody there. That is outdoors, any hour of the day or night. It may be just a bum, but it is somebody. Staying at the Royalton Hotel was nice. A quiet hotel and reasonable. Just off the main drag. It was nice to walk down Broadway and look at the people and sights. On one occasion I was accosted by a young lady, Maggie, who started to give me a spiel. Remembering the time in Texas I asked her if she was selling magazine subscriptions. At that question her expression fell very noticeably. Then we got to talking on the sidewalk. She pointed out two of her co-workers when they passed by. She had just come up from Atlanta. "That was a terrible place. They had a law against girls being found in fellow's hotel rooms". She did not like the idea of being thrown in jail when she only went up to a room to play cards. She had been married. However, since the groom had also been a little underage, his parents had the marriage annulled. Now she was a few months pregnant. They still loved each other deeply. She had only taken this job until her husband got back and they could get remarried.

Just about then Stan came up. We had gone through RTU(Radar Training Unit) together. We exchanged greetings. Maggie said she wanted to see Stan alone for a minute. I told him strictly on the QT that she sold magazines. He thanked me and went into conference. After the conference we went to have a drink together. In the early evening I saw Maggie again and we both nodded hello. She was hanging on the arm of a naval officer.

About the fourth day it was vice-versa and Paul suggested that we come back. So we ate at Peter's house before going back to the field on the next fast freight train.

We finished our week of radar schooling and were to make preparations for aerial flights. Most of us then had Radar Operator entered on our records. The next week they posted shipping lists. Each day they took big bites out of those available. Saturday was the occasion of a heavy date in town even though I came back to camp to sleep. Arrangements had already been made for Sunday and it was just my luck that right after waking at eleven o'clock the phone rang. One of the fellows called my name. While getting up to answer the phone I tried to figure out who it possibly could be. However glum I may have felt, my personal arrangements hit bottom as soon as that information was digested. I had just been assigned to another crew to replace their navigator, who was in the hospital. He had replaced their original navigator who was also hospitalized. As long as there was no reason for not going to the hospital overseas was the next stop. Was there a wish to go overseas? And interrupt having a real good time. Besides I surely did not want to leave the original crew. The Operations Officer said that he would see about that little matter. Anyway it was important to report to the flight line the following morning to start checking out the plane.

The next day we accumulated a great deal of information. Paul's crew was assigned the ship Fare Lady and Bub's name was added. Everyone wondered what Bub was like but that was only a small item. The three other crews that had been assigned to Fare Lady had complained bitterly. Things always seemed to be going wrong with it. The first crew had been replaced because of the navigator taking sick. The navigator of the second crew took sick and the third crew took over. When that navigator decided that he too was sick they decided to replace the navigator until I got there. The four crews on the list directly ahead of Paul's name had been skipped. We never found out why. Since I had asked to stick with my crew they took my crew with me. That satisfied everyone else that had requested a change. But I certainly did not want to feel that I was in any way responsible for my crew drawing an earlier shipping date. Although it was mentioned only once after that. Paul remarked that it was just as well we drew Fare Lady because West had been assigned to the same project number. Otherwise the buddies would have been separated. Peter, the co-pilot was none too happy.

Since none of the ship's instruments had been calibrated that had to be done immediately. The first and easiest job was aligning the drift-meter. One of the crew drew lines on the ground to match the instrument lines along the longitudinal axis of the ship. Then we flew over the local river and went at different speeds to check the airspeed indicator. West came along because he said he knew the pylons marking the ends of the course. However, by the time we finished, that was still a question. Besides, I may have computed wrong and there was an error in calibration. When it came to the compass on the trip back to the field, that was still another story.

I wanted to use the sun to calibrate the compass. Everything was supposed to be set. The time was checked and pencil and paper and assistance were all ready. The data settings were placed on the astro-compass and the astro-compass was placed in the mount. Except that the astro-compass would not go in the mount. After trying to force it, it became obvious that the middle screw used to fasten the mount was 1/8" too long. So we could not swing/calibrate the compass. Paul entered it on the Form 1 along with bum bomb bay doors. I mentioned it to one of the mechanics who said that he would take care of it. When the plane was checked as ready for its next flight the middle screw on the astro-compass mount had not been changed.

We finally got the astro-compass screw fixed and we were all set to leave. At least that's what the record showed.

20/SO LONG, GOODBYE, FAREWELL MORRISON FIELD, FLA MAY 1944

That first afternoon en route we saw our landing field amongst the very flat terrain. There were a number of good-sized lakes in the vicinity. We could see West Palm Beach just on the coast, looking scrupulously clean in the sunlight. It was not very wide but it seemed to stretch for many miles. We checked with the ground personnel at Morrison Field after landing and they did not seem too eager to go into town. Too much on the expensive side for them. Here we were treated very well. They checked our equipment and gave us whatever we needed. They did not have sunglasses though and Paul complained to one of the Tech Sgts. wearing glasses behind the counter. He countered by saying that he had already completed his tour and had kept his glasses. Which ended that. They did not check off that I was supposed to get a watch. I reminded them and they referred the case to the Major in charge. He looked up the records and said that I was supposed to get a watch but now I would have to pay for it. Which left me with about ten dollars. Although there was not any place to really spend it. We did visit the P.X. and get rid of a good part of our remaining moneys. Purchasing whole boxes of candy, cartons of blades and bars of soap. Not knowing whether or not they were hard to get but figuring that they would be useful in any event. There was a very nice swimming pool for the Officers with beach chairs, canopy and all.

When the rest of the crew came to visit us we told them to change in our rooms and come out swimming. So Gene, Rodney, Charlie, Tommy and Bill came swimming. The others came around later. As we saw Paul approach I reminded the fellows that we were going to cross the equator and on board the plane there would not be any chance to dunk the Captain. So I voiced the brilliant idea that we should scare Paul and pretend that we were going to dunk him now. The rest of the crew went for the idea so eagerly that there was a question that it would stop with Paul in a dry condition. We ran over and picked him up bodily and carried him over to the edge of the pool. But we stopped short at the very edge of the pool.

The next day we got our shipping orders and went to a very nice party in the Officers' Club. They had these parties regularly every week. Free food and free soft drinks and there were plenty of women—with the other/permanent Officers.

All along the trip we got briefings. Every time we turned around we got briefings. They all ran pretty much alike. First we were told what course we should fly and then what the weather would be like and then what we should watch out for. Such watching out included ground activities too. We were told that if we had not gotten V.D. around our overseas training bases that we probably would not get it. Because the most concentrated areas for infections were right around those O.T.U.'s (Overseas Training Units). Therefore either we had learned to be careful or we were still abstaining. We were also warned to be very careful of what we ate outside of the States. To make damn sure that what we ate was clean. As most of the foreign countries still had the custom of, to use the vernacular: "Crapping on the Crop". The quickest way to get the G.I.'s was to eat products of such fields. "G.I.'s" is also another name for diarrhea otherwise known as the Delhi Belly, Egyptian Eruptions, Yangtze Rapids etc. depending on your locality at the time. (Of course, in the hospital, G.I. refers to the Gastro Intestinal Ward.) We were briefed to fly from Natal to Dakar. The A20 pilot we had in our midst at one briefing was scheduled to stop at Ascension Island. When we heard that there was an A-20 pilot everyone started to clap. He finally got up and took a bow. The way everyone acted you would think that they were very, very jealous.

At another briefing, the weather officer, who told us what to look for to recognize our landing field when Peter piped up to ask what checks the pilot had in case the navigator fouled up. It caught all the crews and myself with our mouths wide open. I was upset, but I guess it was just his idea of a joke.

21/GOING ABROAD HITHER AND THITHER MAY/JUN 1944

The navigators were handed instructions on the weather we would encounter in the Tropics. One of the things that was pointed out was that the heavy build-up of clouds that might go over ten thousand feet were not the same as the clouds that looked the same over the United States. Near the Equator the clouds did not have the same substance/density as we were familiar with. But it was still better not to enter them and use instruments only. The ship was kept well supplied with aerosol bombs. These were to be used after every takeoff and before every landing. It was supposed to be a good cure for crabs, also to use Scat (mosquito repellant) after dark. We were instructed to keep ourselves covered. Luckily, the air fields we stayed at were all very clean to protect our health.

We passed over the island chain on the way to South America. Late afternoon of June 1 we ran into very thin cloud formations and a little storm. Since the weather was closed in pretty well and the gas did not seem to be holding up it was decided to skip the next dog-leg from Martinique and head for Santa Lucia directly. I was asked for a direct course to the island. After the new course was given to Paul it was decided that it better be verified as much as possible. As we approached our ETA, Paul kept descending. I crawled into the nose turret and kept contact with Paul. It wasn't very light amongst the clouds. The peaks of the clouds were higher than we were flying. Shortly after that, when we did break through the clouds, the faint outline of the island became visible. Santa Lucia sure looked beautiful only a few miles away. We just happened to be lined up with the runway which could not have been more convenient and everyone breathed a deep sigh of relief. It was one of those instances where we felt we were only running on the gas fumes from the gas tanks.

There wasn't much to do that evening so we just reported in to the weather and operations offices. They found beds for us and we made ourselves comfortable. We then walked around the shore and the PX high on the hill but there wasn't much in the PX. Along the beach some of the crew emptied their 45's doing a little target practice. Then we changed our locality in case there were any MP's on the island. Then we went to town, actually it was like a village being a run down collection of huts. A number of the natives accosted us. Mostly they were pretty young girls on the make. Actually the girls were so full of open sores, probably from mosquito bites etc. that most people would be repulsed and we were.

Then along came a couple of MP's in a jeep and ever so politely informed us that GI's were not allowed inside the village limits until after one o'clock. We figured that was so some of the soldiers would get their work done, as a few would no doubt just have moved into the village for the duration. The natives didn't appear too clean but after a prolonged stay they would no doubt look better to the permanent personnel there.

The next morning Paul was obliged to check with Operations regularly for possible clearance. The weather finally cleared in the afternoon and a B-17 landed on its way back to the States.

We went over to look at it. It was inscribed with GI's names from nose to tail. There were also a good many patches on it. That was the first plane that we saw coming back and we were very much interested and pestered the crew with a lot of questions. They answered them willingly enough, undoubtedly glad that they were in a position to do so.

We cleared Santa Lucia that afternoon. The next stop was Trinidad. As we established radio contact and the winds and weather kept shifting the field alternately closed and opened. The crewmen had all been warned about mistaking the clouds for islands on the high seas. The shadow effect is dangerously similar. By this time I'd found that the best way was to spot the waves and whitecaps breaking on the islands' shores.

As we approached Tobago Island I pointed it out to Paul and Peter. There was a little white fringe around part of the edge. Then half an hour later we spotted the real Tobago and still the first clouds and shadows looked like an island even though we now knew that it wasn't. Instructions were to circle around East, South and then West. By then, that approach should be clear. We did and it was.

The next dog-legs were right over the continent of South America. We crossed plenty of what looked like well nigh impenetrable jungle. I was still going almost exclusively by pilotage. Since only the driftmeter had been checked correctly I didn't rely very much on the instruments. Paul kept checking me by radio. To which I didn't pay any attention. About the only time I took over the radio was to check our position at Cayenne. The city itself was under a large cloud that came to a point way above us. Then the radio acted as if it was under the influence of static electronics, induced by the weather.

At Belem, Brazil, we collected a few souvenirs, notably cowboy boots for $5.00 and alligator wrist bands for fifty cents. The boots became quite the rage of all the crewmen passing through. We were disappointed in Rodney. He absolutely refused to buy a pair of boots. Even after I talked to him. I had to borrow a fin from Paul to get mine. Each of us had at least one watch so we didn't purchase any.

At Natal we made a very careful resume of our gas mileage. Then we ran over to Operations to see about the last checkup given our plane and also to find out a few things. We had been regularly checking our gas all the way from the States to see just what margin we were operating on for the long hike across the drink. And the results were not good. We were using approximately 140 gallons per hour in flight. The others were averaging about 110. In order to safely cross the drink we had to average no more than 120 gallons per hour. We were a quite concerned. The Ops (Operations) officer checked a few things about Paul's procedure. It developed that the SOP (Standard Operating Procedure) engine temperatures were now about 20 degrees higher than when Paul had been taught. Therefore he was cruising in RICH throttle more than necessary. That was supposed to account for the excessive consumption of gas. We all hoped that was all but we didn't feel too confident about it. The Engineering Officer informed him that the engine temperature had again been set upward so as to operate hotter. He then assured us that the difference in setting and temperature would give us a safe enough margin of consumption for the trip.

Theory is fine on paper but we weren't very eager, I can tell you, to see if it would work out after we were airborne. We were more than just curious. So Paul had me figure out the halfway point and we would keep a close watch on our gas consumption. Then we would be in a more definite position to tell whether we should continue or not.

The driftmeter was still the only instrument that had been properly aligned or calibrated. I let Paul and Peter play with the radio as usual. The only thing that we could really depend on were the stars. They would have to be used exclusively. My astrocompass could be set up but we would have to know where we were to check the compass. That would also take an assistant. We were to take a course of about 55 degrees and change it to 52 degrees gradually as we went along. An hour out I took a sighting on an island just off the continent. We still had about four hours of darkness. Within the next three hours I took three three-star position fixes (with the sextant). Figuring each one out was just routine and at the end of about the fourth hour I gave a course correction. That was all. I could have gone to sleep for all the good it did. After that we still had six to seven hours to go.

Our trip was planned for a careful check at the halfway mark. The Ops officer said that they hadn't lost a plane in the drink for over a year.

He asked for two volunteers to make a weather report of the entire trip to send back to Natal upon landing. Peter offered to send back the requested weather reports. We took off just as the stars came out. The stars moved west as we went east. Therefore it was necessary to change the stars for each celestial shot for each fix or position location. The first hour out I got a ground speed from the last speck of land we saw in the Western Hemisphere. Fernando Noronha island had a lighthouse which we saw only as a pinpoint in the distance. In the next three hours I took three three-star fixes and plotted them. They checked very closely with the metro wind and heading. After that there wasn't much that could be done. Most of the crew were having a nice comfortable sleep. We kept up continuous radio contact which didn't help us determine our exact position. The briefed altitude was 9,000 feet but we wound up at around 12,000 feet because we kept climbing to keep above the clouds that we saw directly in front of us. Strangely enough we also did have some turbulence on our course.

    At the halfway point I called Paul. We had used up over half of our gas. There was such an obvious reluctance in their attitude to turning back that it was amusing. We knew that we would use less gas for the second half of the trip because of the decreased weight due to the large amount of gas that we had burned up. So unless we hit a headwind which was not expected there would be no problem. The first two-thirds of the trip we had almost a direct crosswind. It was sort of anonymously unanimous that we continue the flight.

    As dawn came up there was nothing we could use for navigation. When the sun came up we could only get a single LOP (line of position) which only tells a portion of the story (either course or ground speed but not position). When the moon is at its highest point in the sky (mean noon) it is possible to get a fix. But only at that moment. I tried to keep shooting to find out when the sun hit its highest point. As a result I shot a total of one and one-half hours (time actually looking into the sextant—figured on the basis of discarded disks—at two minutes each) trying to find the zenith time of the sun. I evidently did not do so good because it came out wrong. So that was that.

    As we approached the coast of Africa, Paul had me figure out the course for a landfall. There wasn't any question that we were on course so he thought we might as well get additional practice on landfalls. Probably he felt best remembering the time we came in over Charleston from the Bahamas using that method. Even though I told him that landfalls were not that accurate. So about an hour from our destination we turned right (east) to approach the west coast of Africa. I used the star from my last fix. There had been a wind shift which was not in the metro and I hadn't caught. It had effectively decreased the ground speed. There was also a very thick haze over the water. We were supposed to be over the coastline at ten minutes after the hour. At twelve minutes after the hour I started to wonder what I would do if our gas ran out. At thirteen minutes after I was beginning to get very concerned. At fourteen minutes after I decided that as long as I had not consciously done anything wrong and as long as worrying wasn't going to help I might just as well stop sweating and see what would happen in case I had to do some fast figuring.

At seventeen minutes after the hour we sighted land. I was in the nose turret as we came into the middle of a large bay or inlet with land on three sides. Being at the center of the bay when we sighted land, our approach wound up just a few minutes off the original ETA. We were then at an altitude of about one hundred feet. Because of the haze it was a good thing that we had kept flying lower to keep contact with the water/ground. We almost certainly would not have seen the coastline at an altitude of 9,000 feet. We also had to fly a little longer than expected because of the wind shift. We made a left turn to fly north, parallel to the coast to Yof (Near Dakar) and come back a little to land there.

After we landed and conferred with the other crews, we found that they had pretty much maintained their altitude and had clear sailing. The next day Paul told me that Shane, another navigator, had given his pilot an ETA (Estimated Time of Arrival) that was right on the button. I was very curious because it had been Shane. Anybody else probably might have done it without too much luck. Shane had bickered with a few of the fellows before he left Charleston and as a result had been changed to his present crew. The causes were quite trivial and it was one of the few cases where members had been changed by request. Usually nothing was done other than express some sympathy for the pilot. I went over and complimented Shane and asked him how he did it. It was all very simple. He said he just kept giving his pilot ETA's until they arrived so the last one was right on the button.

The next day we were scheduled to fly again. I was still pretty tired from so much sextant shooting the previous day. Bub, the bombardier had been bragging so long and loud about how good a navigator he was, that we agreed to let him do the navigating and I would take the pilot's seat after take-off for the trip. We took off and got back over the water on a course almost parallel with the coast. In about ten minutes we could no longer see the coast when we were supposed to be over land. The bombardier suggested I come back in the nose and set him up in business. I did that but we had already lost the information from the first dog-leg. About an hour later we tried it again but I was so fatigued that I gave up trying to fly the plane and just sat in the seat. Then I went back to the nose and directed the plane into destination. And for ever after did the bombardier hold his peace about how good a navigator he was. I was disappointed. It meant that I couldn't goof off.

On our approach into Marrakech we had to pass over some mountains. I told the pilot that after the next valley he should make a turn to the right and come right into destination. He turned the plane right after I finished talking. I figured that he knew where he was and therefore had full control. Later it turned out that he thought I was referring to the valley immediately below us. As a result I lost exact track of our position and we wound up climbing 12,000 feet over the mountains instead of going through the pass. The field lay in a large dust colored valley. The bottom was very flat and dry but surrounding it in the distance were high mountains on every side.

As did all the African cities, the white limestone, or whatever it was, looked very clean in the town buildings from the air. We looked at towns that appeared so clean and figured that was really good. But when we landed and walked through the towns it was very disappointing to find dirt and filth to be the rule and not the exception. In each one of the African towns we visited they had a separate section for special activity. At first we thought it was the name of a town but it only turned out to be the harem or red-light district. And it was off-limits. A number of the fellows had some time previously gotten drunk and been rolled in that part of Marrakech. They tried to give us a good scare when they told us about it—before they gave us passes into town. Those that had come with us left the next day while we had to wait over for one day while the plane was being fixed, because of the same old trouble with the bomb bay doors. We had heard rumors that our plane was sent across before and had been sent back to be fixed before. We waited in Marrakech a whole week for the weather to clear. I got a good rest then.

The other six days we spent looking at the weather each morning. About the fourth day more planes starting coming in. We asked them why they had waited and not left Natal the day after we did. They said that Natal had gotten such a bad report on weather conditions that it was considered advisable to wait three days. That gave us a good laugh because they were referring to our weather report that we had radioed back. We had actually gone through a good deal of weather but the other planes in our flight had not. They had maintained the original altitude so we saw things that they had missed. There wasn't much difference. We just piled up more instrument time for Paul's white instrument card even though he neither desired nor needed it. We all had plenty of confidence in the plane's strength in weather and we had lots of confidence in Paul's taking care of the plane.

Upon leaving we were told to fly along the northern coast of Africa. Also that we should make a 360 degree right turn when we passed a bay near Algiers for identification to the British. Otherwise they would pop us. Then that was called off.

Toward the end of our flight Lt. West and his crew joined us. We both left and flew formation. I had a sore tail and didn't care to navigate. Paul told me not to work so much and I acquiesced. I set up the astro-compass to check the compass on our headings. The shadow of the sextant support fell right on the shadow bar and stayed there for hours. I finally decided to let it go. The plane flew 3 degrees right of our planned course. I checked in a radio beam and figured we were right on course. Barry, on the other plane must have used the same beam. Only it wasn't directional. I didn't pay much attention to it although the co-pilot verified it. Shorty went way off on his calculations with the radio beam and wound up calling for a QDX (position report). That was as if he took the navigators' theme song to heart: "Let's Get Lost".

My ETA was fine except for one small item. There wasn't any field below us. I told Paul to turn left. He contacted the field and they said we were right of course. I then estimated that the compass was off five (5) degrees on that last heading. We flew left about fifteen minutes to the field after that particularly long leg. This time no one ribbed me because I had taken it easy on orders and of course there was no real danger. We continued on to Tunis. Being on a rough coastline, it was easy to spot.

The next stop was in Italy, past Sicily. The middle and northern part of the island were covered by clouds. Paul couldn't follow the briefed route. The southeastern part of the island partially resembles a shelf. There's a plateau where the level drops sharply and then goes out before it dips into the sea. The shelf effect combined with changing directions constantly, fooled me. I mistook Mt. Etna for just another hill. And we kept heading for it. Even at our high elevation it soon became obvious. Since Peter had first raised the question he was the last to let it drop. He loved to lord it over me in such instances. Of course I like to think that there were not enough such cases to satisfy him.

We crossed over Taranto and headed north. Then a real race was on. There were loads of check points and they all had to be noted. If a city went by there was no telling which one we were over. There were so many small cities visible. It was also difficult to tell which were not on the map. Here it was that one could really appreciate American maps. We landed at Gioia Airfield and Paul was immediately relieved of the plane, so it could be sent back. We were put up in cots for the night. After evening chow we decided to go into town. Our first Italian town. Primera Citta de Italia. The Red Cross Club was nice and sociable. Charlie had a good time using his French on the French hostess. The line for ice cream was about a block long. It moved steadily but didn't get any smaller until they ran out of ice cream.

Homer and Omar and their engineer came by from Foggia, our combat base to pick us up and deliver us. In emptying Fare Lady we found a carton of K rations (used for field/combat) that had been put on for our use. They also told us to take the kits along (engineer, radio and such). Rodney wouldn't touch the radio kit so Omar and I did. The tools came in handy later in putting up our tents.

22/REPORTING FOR DUTY FOGGIA, ITALY JUNE 1944

Leaving Gioia on 12 June 1944 we rode with Homer and Omar. We had to notice their nonchalant handling of the plane, which we assumed was how they did it in combat. Although we did consider them a little unnecessarily rough on the controls.

At Castellucia we did not seem particularly welcome. They did not even have tents for us. They were in the process of building an orderly room. It only had the roof and walls. We bedded down on the dirt floor that first night. The windows had not been installed but that was not so bad, it was summer. During the winter, before the main equipment arrived, everyone was wearing full flying suits to sleep in. It was the best way to keep comfortably warm. The next day we were very eager to learn when we were going to fly our first combat mission. We may not have been eager to fly it but we were very eager to learn when we were going to fly.

The C.O., Major Miner, decided that we were to erect our own tents. So we got two good tents or the canvas and wood that go to make them up. We officers picked a nice spot for ours (not too convenient to the orderly room, of course). Then we went over to help the enlisted men (or at least to watch them). After all, an officer's first job is to see that his enlisted men are taken care of (even if they have to do it themselves). We helped them hit a stake in here and there and gave suggestions freely (which they were too smart to follow). After they had done a fairly good job and we had gotten the benefit of their experience we set up our own tent and invited them over to watch. They did come over and they did watch too. One of them even picked up a hammer but we got it back.

After the tent was set up we went to work on the cots and mosquito netting. Yes, mosquito netting. I fashioned two wooden sticks for mine. The pieces were fashioned so that clothes could be hung over the vertical sticks. I hung my helmet on one of them. The others all laughed and pointed out the resemblance to the crosses over graves with the helmets on. So I finally changed it. Of course, I am not superstitious, I just believe that for the same price you might as well have superstition on your side.

Here was really roughing it in combat. We washed and shaved with water in our helmets. We used our canteens to carry and keep the drinking water. Had to use outdoor plumbing—country style. They used plain ordinary wood for seating reinforced with tin. It was not anywhere as popular as the States' version—after a short time, two seconds or so, one's seat became uncomfortably corrugated. So everyone read books and magazines in the comfort station.

The maps they gave us sure made us appreciate the ones we had in the States even more. I flew off the field almost a dozen times before I realized that the airfield was misplaced on the map. Three miles off. I wondered why I didn't come out where I expected, at first. But the thing that really put me on the track was when I started to walk east to town and was told that the nearest town was west. The pilots, of course did not have any trouble. They did not use any maps in combat. So they could spot the field from the air much quicker. After that it was not safe to take anything on the maps for granted.

A small old building was converted into a shower room. A tank was hoisted up to the level of the top of the building and water was piped through four outlets. Officers alternated days with enlisted men. It was particularly crowded right after missions and during the summer before evening mass. There was not any other means of washing completely. Some Eye-ties that worked at the camp would solicit laundry work. They would then bring it home for their wives to do. They could not count the pieces too well all the time, so some of the fellows were sometimes short-changed. I had gotten name-tapes through Bobby and here I sewed them on all my clothes that were laundered. After that I did not miss a single item. I did not bother to count after that.

Each person was issued a PX ration card. Squadron Supply got rations each week for issue to the Officers and Men. The rations included soap, razor blades, matches, 8 to 10 packages of cigarettes (or a half-dozen cigars), two cokes and five bottles of beer per week. A can of fruit juice every other week. Also, if you could lay your hands on a cigarette lighter, watch or pen and pencil set, you were entitled to keep one of them.

I had always managed to have the same PX girl wait on me. Not just because she was the prettiest but we enjoyed talking in Italian. She would not go out with me. Her fidenzera (fiance) would not approve of it. Also, we never knew far enough ahead of time when we were going to fly and when we were not for me to make any plans three or four days in advance. In spite of the fact that for my stay in Italy I only averaged one mission a week as a member of a lead crew.

Anyway, the PX got Ronson lighters one day. This girl asked me if I needed fiamiferri (matches). So I bought some matches. Then she showed me that she meant the lighters. Very nicely chrome-plated and an attachment for wind-proofing. I immediately bought it. Nobody ever mentioned seeing either watches or pen and pencil sets come in. They were shipped out all right. They were just too valuable to let get out of hand. When the Squadron got a shipment of about six knives, they raffled one off for the whole Squadron. Now don't tell me you don't know what happened to the other five. There were more than five guys that worked in supply alone. The Officers took their chances on first come, first served at the PX in town. By the time I got back to the Squadron all the lighters were sold out. I was offered a profit at once, which I refused. There was lighter fluid available. Paul always filled his with the 100 octane gas which had a tendency to evaporate. He used to have Walter fill it by tapping one of the gasoline line outlets in the bomb bay.

About the third day Paul was scheduled with another crew. But it was a stand-down (no fly). The next day the same thing happened. The day after that they scheduled the whole crew together. So we excitedly got up in the morning with the other crews. It really was in the middle of the night, they schedule take-offs for right after dawn. Just enough light to see the other planes on the runway. We rushed down to the mess hall for breakfast and caught the truck for briefing at group headquarters. They dished out sheets for the pilots and navigators which were called poop sheets. Poop from Group they called it. There we learned the target for the day, the route to and from, what opposition we might encounter (any relation to actual was accidental), where we would meet with what kind of escort and to maintain radio silence except in cases of dire emergency. The opposition or expected gunfire from the enemy was only stated for the whole area of combat. Therefore, what one might run into on each mission could be far more or less than the average/expected flak and/or gunfire. Our crew learned that process pretty thoroughly before we actually took off. We repeated the briefing process six times before our first combat mission.

We just finally got tired of being excited, apprehensive and keyed up for nothing. Usually the first pilot flies with another crew to get experience. In our case, they flew us from our first combat mission till the crew was broken up, by Paul's being retired from combat. In the meantime we had only minor substitutions. Our crew worked very well together up in the air. Even on the ground there was a minimum of friction—just enough to keep us as being real normal people. Even when some of the gunners were scheduled every day for a month, like Tommy, he became very much on edge at the time, but that was all. We still got along fine. It was more than twice as bad for Bill when one of the waist gunners got hit. As ball gunner he got to bandage the wounded man. The wounds were usually very ugly and Bill was shaken later, but at the time he really did a good job.

Things eased up for him after a number of missions and he got a rest for a few days. The operation was very short of ball gunners and tail gunners.

Navigators and Bombardiers too. It seemed to be a practice to give the pilots the Distinguished Flying Cross and the Navigators and Bombardiers the PH degree (Purple Heart). For Squadron Navigators and Bombardiers it was a little different though—they usually got the DFC. But that was combat. Live and get promoted. Every mission consisted of about one-third leaders, one-third deputy leaders and one-third followers. But things were changed about so much amongst the smaller units that it did not amount to much. Only the Squadron Leaders and such rated beans.

    Our first mission was a lulu, a real initiation. The target was in Italy with little or no flack expected. We flew on somebody's wing. The lead pilot flies in the middle with one plane on each wing and the second tier is stepped down, each in a "V" shape. That day we flew in the second tier. Following any leader is called flying off his wing because that is the relative position. The pilot or co-pilot, whoever is farther away has to fly cross-cockpit and they relieve each other regularly so they do not get stiff necks. Any such effort at altitude is multiplied strain at 20,000 feet. The leaders must keep their throttle adjusted as close to the briefed airspeed as possible. When conditions permitted it, the leader flew on automatic pilot. Usually the wing and sometimes the group lead planes would set their throttles and everyone took positions on them. By the time throttle settings got to "Tail-End Charlie", he has to change his setting so often he might not take his hand off the throttle. At 160 miles per hour, one mile more or less does not seem so much. But when measured across fifty feet from death with smashed wings, its a rather delicate adjustment. Imagine setting a car throttle at fifty miles an hour (even on a level road) and following another car with a ten foot margin. How close can the average driver stay?

    We took off in the proper position and followed our element leader to join up with his flight which joined the Group and then the Wing. I tried navigating from the flight deck—just in back of the pilot and co-pilot and sometimes used the radio operator's desk. I had been told that this was the best position. It was impossible to see the instruments from the desk and the top turret got in the way. It was very difficult to write standing up. So I did not have a very good log. We flew north over the Adriatic and spotted our target beneath some broken (not solid) clouds. At the IP (initial point—start of the bomb run) the bombardier set up his bomb-sight although he was to drop on the leader('s signal). Just about that time we noticed little black puffs expanding in the air below us.

In all innocence we were very interested. We assumed that it was flak. Sure enough, it was. But nowhere close enough to do any damage. We opened the bomb-bay doors as did the others and went on the target run. After passing over the target we repeated the performance from another angle, then another. After flying around in that vicinity awhile we left and flew south. This was not strictly according to Hoyle. But the crew figured that maybe the target was just a little too covered by clouds to get a direct hit on it. Anyway we flew back across the Adriatic and back over northern Italy, still over enemy territory. Spotting something, we made a 270 degree (heading) run on another target. It looked like we hit it good only the pictures might not have agreed with the report. When we got back to the field they called a meeting of the bombardiers. At that report at Group it was said that the lead navigator got lost and thought he was bombing the original target. I did not see how such a thing could possibly have happened but then I was so green. When S2 (Intelligence) asked us what our heading was on the bombing run I said 90 degrees, which is the reciprocal of what it had been. And our instructors had warned us so much about reciprocal headings—if they could only have been with me then.

The first time we were scheduled to go to France it was overcast. In coming up through the overcast we lost the rest of our element. Everyone was keeping watch to sight any other planes above the clouds. We spotted one and then another. After making some very large circles over the rendezvous area we left to follow the briefed course. That took us west to the coast. By that time one of the planes we saw turned out to be West's crew. We conversed on interphone. We were sure that our Group had not beat us to the coast and let a few groups pass us to check them. We did a few S turns over the coast and then Paul spotted another group of planes approaching. We did a 360 turn to give them time to get to us. West stayed right with us. The others that we picked up went across the sea with other groups to complete their mission. Just as we were finishing our turn back to the course this other group approached us. However the pilot's face got red as the B-24's approached and turned out to be P-38's. What I considered the classic of them all happened in the shower. We had just acquired a half dozen new crews and they were being sent out on the easy missions to France. We thought that was a pretty bad way to break them into combat flying. They would think that they knew what it was all about and become overconfident. The best insurance was still to expect the worst. That way you saved time that you might otherwise use up being surprised and could therefore react much more quickly. Anyway one of these new crews came into the shower after a mission to France. Probably their first mission, too. They had even seen flak. Now when flak explodes it has a sort of cross between a pod-pod and a crunching sound. When it hits the plane it sounds like gravel on a tin roof. When it goes through the plane it screeches and whistles like any other projectile. The fragments have very rough edges that leave particularly nasty holes. One of the new pilots was heard to remark: "Boy, was that flak close". One of the old timers casually asked: "Could you hear it hit?" The first pilot replied: "No, we could not hear it, but it was too damn close for comfort".

We were beginning to think that the fourth mission scheduled was getting to be routine. At group we learned the target was in Germany. Everyone was laughing in falsetto. They even had to use a big ladder to reach it on the target map. That was the first time the Colonel used real horsesense. He gave orders to carry a little extra with our escape kits. And especially, when we were coming back, just before we ran out of gas, to select a good spot to crashland or ditch the plane. That made us feel even better to know that the Colonel was not going to hold us responsible for bringing the planes back.

We went back to our tent and loaded up a barracks bag for ourselves. We dumped clothes and food and equipment into it. Anything we thought might come in handy. Then dragged it out to the plane. Everyone sweated out a takeoff time and kept their good eye on the tower. With minutes to go the tower released two red flares. The noises and yells of exultation could be heard across the pits. Half the planes released red flares to celebrate. We felt tremendously relieved and yet we did not know what we had really missed.

Rocko came into the orderly room once in a while. He had over a hundred missions, two DFC's, a DSC, NSS, a PH and I can't remember how many AM's and theatre ribbons and stuff. They were all on his record too. I took a letter to the Officers' PX for him to get the ribbons once. He had been in the Asiatic-Pacific area, completed a tour in Africa, a tour in England, and was now finishing a tour in Italy. Said he had gotten the Silver

Star for landing a B-24 in Africa when his officers had gotten shot up. Came in at right angles to the runway with two flat tires. He had also fallen out of the plane once on takeoff. His heavy flying clothing had prevented him from getting hurt. He had trouble sleeping at night—talked incessantly in his sleep and rocked and tossed. Maybe you're wondering why he didn't quit. Well, his brother and father had been killed in the war. He'd soldiered under his father, a Major, in the States.

Rocko regularly operated a waist gun. On one mission he had dropped his mike and bent down to pick it up. When he straightened up there were two flak holes directly in line with the upper half of his body. The last time we saw him he had just gotten out of the hospital and was limping. He had stopped a piece of flak that had nicked him in a sensitive and unmentionable place and then lodged in his leg. He looked like he needed a rest and I asked him about it. But no, he was back on flying status and was due to be scheduled at any time.

We had a lot of discussions with and about Bub. He had told us that he was definitely going to be a lead bombardier. He was not going to stop at his total missions required either. He was going to do one hundred missions, he did not mind altitude. Why on practice missions he had always been willing to fly at the highest briefed altitudes. The first mission he turned on the bombsight and used it. The second mission he only turned on the bombsight. By the third mission he was having a terrific amount of trouble with his ears at altitude. The he confided to us that he had always had trouble. Even on practice missions. Sure enough, it was on his record but nobody cared to check. The last mission he flew he had slumped over the bombsight and I could not tell if he had passed out or not. So just as a safety measure I turned his oxygen supply on to full emergency. Figuring that if he did not like it he could easily turn it off. He regained consciousness just in time to drop the bombs on target. After that he acted like I had saved his life and I could then do no wrong. The flight surgeon took him off flying status. He was sent to Headquarters at Bari for six months. Major Miner said that he would like to get him back at the end of six months. What did Bub do at Bari? He had a good time I am sure. It was his job to interrogate American airmen who did not come back the same way they left (by plane).

The next bombardier we then got, Buddy, had been an instructor back in the States. Shortly after this when Paul and I were in the Orderly room, he looked up my record and it read that I was not qualified to be a lead navigator. Paul offered to change that record but I figured that it didn't matter and told him not to. By the time we Extra Joker Officers had gotten about twenty missions our enlisted men had seen an awful lot of action some with thirty or more missions. Our goal was then changed to fifty missions. So although Telly had piled up a few more missions, Paul's crew was selected for a week at rest camp. Telly beefed like mad but orders was orders.

When we finally were assigned to rest camp we were flown to Naples. The AMG Mayor (American Military Governor) was Major Hersh, Sec'y of my Bnai Brith Lodge in Chicago. But there was no time to spend in Naples. We took a boat out to the Isle of Capri. There was a scattering of nurses and WAC's aboard. As we steamed into the beautiful harbor of Capri, one WAC took a look and moaned: "Oh, if this is Capri, I'm taking the next boat back". I told her that was sort of silly, at least give it a day. Two days later I took another look and took the boat back myself.

The island was badly in need of a whitewash. The hotels were nice and modern. Buddy and I insisted on sleeping in the same room. Peter cramped our style and Paul didn't care. Since Capri was an official rest camp we could wear anything instead of our uniforms. Glen and I rushed out to buy shirts with Capri written on them. Got a real silk neckerchief for only three dollars. Other things like handmade combat ribbons were in big demand. Most of us bought a strip of the Air Medal, American Theatre and ETO. Paul bought a strip including the DFC and Purple Heart. No, he had not been awarded those as yet. Anyway they would look good on his battle jacket as soon as he was awarded them. I purchased some necklaces and bracelets with cameos.

When Buddy and I left Capri, Paul and Peter gave two of our crew some insignia so our rooms were not vacant. Buddy and I hit the road for Rome. We got a lift by a Britisher who also picked up some merchant mariners. They were beefing about the lack of privilege accorded them. In Rome I looked up the city directory for Sr. Roberto. Not only that, I found it. Per usual I asked the next pretty girl I saw how to get to his address. She did not know but the gal sitting next to her told us.

I told Sr. Roberto that Glen sent us. We were shown a well furnished spacious room. It had very luxurious rugs and oil paintings. The rates were two dollars for each of us per day and four dollars if we had company. Coming to Rome on orders was a real deal. At first the passes admitted an Officer and his guest. The Americans had requisitioned all the better hotels. Then it was restricted, the guest could not have breakfast in the hotel.

Then the guest could not have lunch. Later we heard that an Infantry Captain had a disagreement with his guest and he had chucked her out of the second story window. It seemed to have had something to do about prices. After that guests were not allowed.

I went on a Red Cross sightseeing tour. The thing that impressed me most was that St. Peter's Cathedral was so beautiful. It was worth the trip alone. Everything about it was just like we had been told and I remembered seeing pictures of it in school. In the yard there were two half circle columns, three deep. Standing on either one of two spots, one of the half circles looked like only a curved line of columns. The second and third rows were so perfectly aligned.

Our guide pointed out the seven hills and the Tiber River. We went through the catacombs and the guide told us about this and that which were now gone. The thing that impressed me secondly was that so much in Rome was missing. It dwelt so much in memory. In spite of the modern building additions.

Then there was the Transient Officers' Mess. The Italian restaurants had to get practically all their food at the black market. The girls preferred only those Officers who had hotel reservations because the food was much better. The magic password was "Mangare" (eat) to interest the girls. The girls struck me as painted dolls because they had so much more makeup on than the ones in the rest of Italy. They promenaded along the street that was lined with hotels. The street vendors had some very nice mosaic pins which I bought. There were different minute designs fashioned of individually colored pieces. Here again, I would have felt like a fool if I had paid their first asked price. I still often felt that my first bid had not been low enough. Leaving Rome we had to hitchhike back to Naples to meet the rest of the crew and transportation back to the field.

Flying Officers were supposed to censor their enlisted mens' mail. But most of the EM's did not appreciate that. Our crew insisted that we sign either their empty or sealed envelopes. As a tease, we insisted on reading their letters but they absolutely refused.

Every so often Buddy would tell us some of the things that came up in the mail room censoring. As, for instance, the time he was reading a passionate and sensual loveletter to Jean. It depicted the things Loverboy would do upon his return when Jean would cook a welcome supper for him and he would smother her with kisses etc., etc. Buddy started to read it to the others when one of them said I have the same thing only this is addressed to Joan. Sure enough, upon comparison the two letters were almost identical, with the exception of the girls' names. After comparison they were very careful, for Loverboy's sake, to get the right letter into the right envelope.

Lt. Luke had come over with the Group. He knew practically everyone of importance. He went on long sightseeing tours of Italy as his fancy directed him. When he did come back he would say when he was to be scheduled. Every once in a while he would put his missions in. If it had not been so serious, it would have been amusing to see some of the changes between the original schedules and the final ones when the target was known.

I had a collection of poems and jokes that I used to add to and type and hand out and send to friends. So I spent some time in the orderly room. I had also brought my harmonica with a few song books and practiced that. I played it in the tent. After a few weeks, either the fellows forgot what good music sounded like or else I improved tremendously, because they once even went so far as to ask me to drag out my harmonica. One of my sisters had sent me one. That I lent to Bill. He really played it good and by ear, too. So I did not let him use my better one in my tent. I always told him that he could keep both of them if I ever got shot down and he didn't.

I also started to study the Italian language having a good start from having taken two years of Spanish in high school. Although I had forgotten most of it, the two languages were very similar. I purchased half a dozen books and studied them. Starting with the primer, the second grade book and third grade book. They had very simple words and pictures which were most helpful. My method was almost strictly from the utilitarian point of view. I concentrated on only a few things. The minimum of useful tenses, names of most common objects, some prepositions and pronouns. I never took a dictionary with me. I preferred to remember the hard way. Many times I took long walks over the surrounding countryside. Foggia province was supposed to be the most fertile section south of the Po valley. The cities may have been unkempt, dirty and full of malaria and such as stripped by the Nazis. But the countryside was luxuriantly green. I walked into a half dozen cities and checked later to find that each of them were off limits. One hundred percent malarial. I would fortify myself with matches, till I got a lighter and pass out cigarettes, with candy for the children, in exchange for fresh fruit and such.

I really enjoyed the long talks with the people I met. There was a comfortable absence of formality, whether I wished to buy produce or just pass the time of day. Mostly when I practiced my broken Italian, they would respond in their broken English. They, of course were very eager for the soap(women) and the cigarettes(men) that I always carried with me. They were not too interested in the money that we were issued. Of course, the Nazis had confiscated property and they sometimes issued German marks that were good for redemption only after the war. Once the Nazis were gone the only use for those marks was as souvenirs. Before the war, a lire was worth four cents. Now it was only worth one cent. But it seemed that they upped their prices about four times on some things. That left the Americans holding the bag. It seemed that at almost every farmhouse or home I stopped at and talked, they had either a relative that lived in America or else a prisoner of war there. In the latter case particularly, they would inquire about the living conditions. I told them the truth that Italian prisoners of war were living better in the States than American soldiers were living in Italy. We had no particular love for the PBS(Peninsular Base Section) which rationed all our food.

Even the truck schedules, to and from Foggia, were not too reliable. There was a definite shortage of vehicles. We had more vehicles in salvage than we did in good running order. It was almost impossible to get hold of a jeep. Before I got there they had no rules against motorcycles. Then the guys kept mixing too much alcohol and gasoline and motorcycles were banned. Some of the guys kept theirs on the QT. Glen and I almost bought one. But I had an aversion to sneaking around on one. Half of the reason I was not eager to become Squadron Navigator was because the position did not even rate a jeep.

There may be a lot of controversy as to whether American vehicles are better than others. My personal opinion is that the combination of American driver and vehicle are much better on the average. As for instance, the time I got a lift in a British light truck. Now, mind you, I certainly appreciated the lift. But in crossing a creek before we got to the main macadam highway, the driver chose to use second gear. Well, we were not going quite fast enough for second gear and started to bog down in the middle of the creek. He then got the bright idea of changing to first gear instead of accelerating in second. Sure enough, just as he slowed up the engine to change gears we bogged down. We waited a short time for a winch truck to pull us out. An American truck, of course.

I came back very hungry from one mission. The mess hall was serving fried spam and cold rich chocolate drink. I had several helpings of both, just filling myself up. I left the mess hall and got about a hundred feet away. Right by the disposal pot. There I just regurgitated but I was not hungry anymore. The stuff just would not mix and stay down in my stomach. Upon being asked what was wrong I honestly replied "Nothing". Circumstantial evidence to the contrary.

The Officers' Club at the field was a two story affair. It was not very spacious. A dance was held there once. Two nurses showed up. Everyone was so disappointed they did not try again. Downstairs was a bar and an Italian radio and a table to play craps on. Upstairs was a reading room with books and magazines and card tables. The Officers helped themselves to the books and magazines which were periodically replenished. A couple of times (twice), I managed to get the monthly GI Hit Kit copy containing words and music. It came in handy with my harmonica.

The Officers got a ration issue of a bottle of whiskey. Only the ground Officers hung around long enough to get a second bottle. It all went into a kitty anyway. Sold over the bar at two bits ($.25) a shot. There were plenty of local drinks available, such as vermouth and vino. However, they were not particularly popular.

Before I say anything more about combat flying I wish to explain a little. I felt that the less of an impression the missions made upon me, the less effect they would have upon my feelings, etc. I made no attempt to remember details. Peter seemed to remember everything about the missions. His hair seemed to turn gray before we were through, too. Rodney wrote down most everything that happened in his little black book. He also wrote home an account. The last time I saw him in Italy there was not any particular change in him. Also, determining how rough combat conditions were was very subjective and often affected by previous experiences.

According to the old-timers the general reaction was from 0 to 15 missions—don't know enough to be afraid. From 15 to 30 missions—really sweat them out. From 30-40 missions—well it's almost over now. From 40 to 50 missions—really sweat them out far more than before. The number of missions to complete a tour in England was fifty to rotate back to the States. Their hump seemed to be the first ten missions. Once those were under their belt there seemed to be a good chance of finishing up – so "THEY" said. Also, being afraid did not necessarily make the crucial difference.

When Major Miner approached his forty missions the Air Corps started bombing southern France in preparation for the invasion. Our crew went on one of those and that was one time that I did not fly with them. Being replaced by a Navigator who was finishing up his last few. It appeared that Major Miner made sure that he went on every one of these milk runs. He was not fussy either. He put himself on as co-pilot of any ship he chose, whether it was #4 or #5 even when he was supposed to be in #1. Telly seemed to have a little trouble getting scheduled then also. But one other pilot didn't, he made sure he maintained his connections with the powers that be.

Debates of all sorts were continuously going on. One in particular was the choice of ditching, crash landing or bailing out. When Homer and Omar did not return from a mission, the whole crew wondered what had happened. After all, they had flown us up here and they were strictly hot pilots. Last seen over the Adriatic. The next day we heard that they had ditched off the coast near Bari. Then two days later we heard that a fishing boat had picked up the crew right after they ditched. They were short of gas from being hit. Two of the crew got killed in the ditching.

I always kept busy on missions except during the bomb run. Then I gave the bombardier lots of room. Only keeping a pencil and the log handy to record time, direction, speed and altitude for "Bombs Away". Twice on missions I became self-conscious of being huddled up on the deck practically praying that the flak did not come any closer. Upon realizing this I concentrated on other things. How much longer till the bombs away? Were there many enemy fighters around. How was the rest of the Group doing? It was not that I did or did not believe in God—I guess I was just being fatalistic.

Peter sometimes had a difficulty breathing, said he had some sort of sinus trouble. He got hold of an inhaler which he always carried around in his pocket and sniffed at regular intervals whether on the ground or airborne. I was lucky not to catch a cold. Nonetheless, on two missions I ran into difficulty. Both times it happened on the return trip about an hour after we had hit the target. I would feel the pressure just like a regular sinus headache. Then it got to the point where my sight seemed weird. I could look but only part of my sight would register. If I wanted to find a something on the map I could look but it was difficult to correlate the spatial relationship. I would look at the map and I would look at the ground and there would be minimal connection or similarity. Yet I knew I was not lost. Both times I called the bombardier from the flight deck to take over. He would navigate for a short while and then I would again take over. The second time it happened I went to the dispensary instead of to interrogation because the cranial pressure was still so great upon landing. The medic sprayed my nose and I could feel it take effect. I then got an inhaler.

The next mission that I felt the same pain in my head at 20,000 feet I used the inhaler. In a few moments the pressure had subsided. I always carried the inhaler with me after that even if I did not use it very much. These two trips on which I was not effective for a short while also weighed on my decision not to buck for Squadron Navigator.

23/EXTRA JOKER ET AL EUROPE JUL/AUG, 1944

At some point on the way overseas, it seems that Paul and Charlie and Peter put their heads together and with the aid of a deck of cards decided that when and if we got a permanent plane assigned to us it would be called Extra Joker.

Early one morning, we got up and went to the briefing as usual. In checking the poop sheet, Paul saw that we had been scheduled for Extra Joker as usual. They had only recently put out an order to the effect that only ships with Norden bomb sights would be used in the lead. That was right up Buddy's alley too. He had been an instructor in Norden and no one else in the Squadron had the majority of their work done with Norden, including the Squadron Bombardier. Paul checked the poop sheet with the Operations Officer so we took another ship. On the poop sheet we were still shown with Extra Joker. But that would now fly in #2 or deputy lead position. We took a brand new un-Christened ship and we were to initiate it on its first mission. The ship was so new that Buddy had not seen that particular Bombardier's instrument panel before and he asked the ground crewman in charge of bombsights to check it with him. The EM told him to turn on all the switches on the bomb run and then drop as usual. The photographer was listed to go on the deputy lead ship according to the poop sheet. Actually, because we switched planes between planning and takeoff the photographer wound up in the #1 position in our lead ship. We Officers were not aware of his presence till after takeoff, that there was an extra man on board.

We assembled as usual to find that instead of having seven ships in our flight we had only three. Four others had already aborted before we got over the Adriatic. So Paul called up the Colonel in the Group lead and suggested that he either give us all the spares so that the strength would at least be 6,6,6,5 instead of the present 7,7,6,3. Or else split up our flight to strengthen the others to 8,8,7. But the Colonel couldn't see it. He told Paul to maintain the present status because he did not expect trouble. Over Yugoslavia one of the other members of our flight caught up. The target was a little flying training field about forty miles west of a usual target. The majority of the Air Corps was hitting all around that area. We saw our fighter escort a couple of times.

As we approached the target, there was a partial undercast and I figured that we were going about five miles off our I.P. (Initial Point). Just about that time we ran into some flak. We no more had time to notice it then the sky was full of enemy fighter planes. We told S-2 later (that means we got back) that there were about 75 planes in the air of alien manufacturers and that fifteen of them lined up at one time to come in at us. Tommy, the tail-gunner got the best view of the attack, at no extra charge. They dove in from our rear. Being the low, low flight they hit us first and hardest. First #4 went down right behind us and then #2 was in the limelight. By this time Walter was so enthused with getting some really good pictures that he may have been paying more attention to see that the photographer was getting some fabulous shots than he was to his waistgun.

Walter was on the right waist gun and he could see #2 which was Extra Joker. It got hit a number of times by 20mm and the photographer took a series of pictures showing the hits, the flames and how they enveloped the whole plane. Then it dropped a few hundred feet off our starboard side and blew up. It looked likely that nobody could have gotten out alive. The pictures that were printed clearly showed the waist gunners and pilot slumped over in an unlifelike position. They might have attacked others better fit for defense if we had not looked so vulnerable. The photographer, Sgt. Berg, got the DFC (Distinguished Flying Cross for the series of thirteen (13) pictures that he took of Extra Joker. The irony of the situation was that the photographer was supposed to be in the #2 plane—Extra Joker.

Buddy got on the bomb-sight all right only when he pushed to drop the bombs nothing happened. And we had fragmentation bombs. They were the most dangerous to handle. It was practically a miracle that nothing hit them and set them off. One of the switches that was "ON" was supposed to be "Off" in order to drop the bombs. So our bombs hung on through all the excitement. Our gunners accounted for a half-dozen of the enemy planes. While we were on the bomb run and I had the log closed so that Buddy would have more room, I looked out the window. As the planes had attacked they came under us and some of them turned on their backs in order to expose only their armor-plated bellies to us. Walter hit two of them but only counted one as definite and one as probable. That was all the effect we could see. He lined up on almost everyone that passed. There was not enough room between them to include every single one. One of the pieces of bullet or shrapnel had passed through the bomb bay and clipped the wires of one of the throttles so that it could be set up but not set back. That was the total extent of our real damage. We joined another flight right after the attack but the whole Group had sustained severe damage. We jettisoned the bombs over Yugoslavia. The #3 plane, off our left wing could not make it back and dropped out of the formation for bailing out. We could only see about five chutes leave the plane. Thus went Makowsky. This was only his second or third mission. He had not even been around long enough to get acquainted with. All we knew was the name from the poop sheet.

The trip back was fairly uneventful otherwise. As much as our ship was hit it did not seem damaged too badly. We could not tell in the air, whether or not the tires had been hit so we braced ourselves on the landing to make sure that if they were flat we would not be jerked too hard. As luck would have it, even the tires were good and Paul made a good landing (as usual). But we sure felt relieved when we got out and touched the ground. We went to see the C.O. about getting the D.F.C. for each enlisted man on the crew. Figuring that if it had not been for them we would not have come back from that trip. But such things just were not done. The C.O. suggested that either he could not put through a report as we told him or the Colonel most certainly would not approve of anything like that intimating that he had fouled us up. The C.O. suggested that either he give the Enlisted Men the "Soldier's Medal" or else the incident just be forgotten. We laughed at getting them the Soldier's Medal because we knew they would not be interested. I think our EM's had the record for the Group for the most enemy planes shot down at that time.

Upon our return from rest camp we learned that our Group was making ferry trips to France and getting credit for combat missions. We figured that was just our luck. A few days later we were scheduled for a ferry mission. Lt. Shore from S-2 asked to come along. He was so excited that it appeared to be his first combat mission. Our path lay over Corsica to about fifteen miles SW of Marseille. Then we turned north to Lyon.

But as soon as we crossed the southern coast of France we began flying between layers of clouds. I just caught a glimpse of a turn of a river about ten miles to the right. I took the metro wind from briefing, the wind from the two headings of the turn SW of Marseille and the checkpoint. I combined these to estimate a single wind. From that I gave Paul the course. We flew North for an hour. I estimated that we were within fifteen miles of Lyons. Paul heard the radio station order all planes back because the field was closed. He turned around and I gave him a course south using the same estimated wind. In the meantime we could see nothing but clouds. I still kept the DR (dead reckoning) figures and also kept looking out. When Paul asked if I could see any checkpoints I told him that the cloud on the right looked familiar. That must have satisfied him, he didn't ask anything more.

We came out over the coast about a mile from where we had left and about a minute off on the ETA. It was decided to land and unload rather than bring the load of gasoline drums back all the way to Italy. So we landed at Aixle, Marseilles. It was only a small landing field and the OC shot us into the town of Aix to feed us.

Here I was amazed. In contrast to the impoverished Italian girls in the small towns around Foggia, each of the girls I saw here had an almost meticulous hair-do. They may not have been a bit prettier but there was so much more apparent pride of personal appearance. It was most probable that the war had not hit anywhere as hard here as at our base in Italy. But the prettied up girls gave it a touch of home. Buddy and Shore had gotten a lift to Marseilles, had gone to a hotel and had a really good time. I had gone to the same Army school with Ralph and now he was a Radar Navigator in another squadron. We found rooms together. I looked all around for Buddy and Shore. We started out for the field together and then we got separated. We did not take the first truck back to the field from town and there was not a second truck. They got back to Aixla-Marseilles after I had left with Ralph and his crew. I got to the field to find that ours was the only crew from our squadron that had already flown back. When they arrived at the home field Major Miner pinned Captain's bars on Paul.

I flew in the nose turret and picked out check points and estimated the wind on the water. He said it was way off. I surprised both of us by differing from Ralph's DR post mortem wind by 10 degrees and 5 miles per hour and being closer to actual.. The next leg over water he gave me his estimated wind and asked my opinion. Since it looked okay to me I said so.

Back at Camp I was still burned up at being left behind. Buddy dismissed the matter lightly. Not only did I not have a good time but I had sweated out their return. There were plenty of other ships waiting and Buddy and Shore had gotten one of those. The next time we flew together it was a short combat trip and my name was on the schedule. Then the Group started flying combat again. They all tried to tell me how much rougher our targets had gotten.

When Buddy was asked what he was doing in combat he loved to relate this story about the bombardier instructor that said: "Its all a mistake, I really had a swell deal as a Bombardier Instructor. I was going with two different girls. Each thought that I flew every other night when I didn't stay with them. When they asked me if I wanted additional schooling for Bombardiering, I said No. If I had said yes, I would still be an Instructor. He almost despaired of being promoted. Fellows that he had instructed would come up to him to say hello and they would be wearing 1st Lt's bars while he still wore 2nd Lt's bars."

Major Miner put Buddy on the hit list when he showed up late for the flight line. Then as far as the Major was concerned, everything Buddy did was wrong. When the Squadron Bombardier was replaced, Troy came in. He was a Sperry man and at that time the Squadron was changing to Norden bombsights. Buddy had instructed Norden and was not only the best, he was the only Norden specialist in the Squadron.

Another mission that I did not fly with Paul and the crew he again led the Group. The night before they talked about the opportunity it would afford Buddy to show Major Miner how good he was if Troy aborted. Paul and Major Miner and Troy flew in the lead ship. Buddy, and I think Telly, flew in the deputy lead. Sure enough, Troy cooperated. He did not check his bombsight till they got to the I.P. Then he looked and saw that the bombsight had been removed. He had to abort and Buddy took over in the bomb run. Set up his sight for lead and prepared to drop. Told the navigator to open the bomb bay doors. It seems that the Navigator did not hear him. The delay caused the first flight bombs to drop two seconds late. The other three flights dropped in time and hit the target. What do you think Major Miner did when the Squadron got back. He berated Buddy for dropping his bombs late. Said it was acting like a pilot coming in for a landing with his wheels up and locked.

I still used to spend some spare time in the orderly room and still kept two separate lists of "literature" for fellows and girls and typed out copies for mailing. One day a Lieutenant walked in and asked: "Where's Lt. Makowski?" I told him that he had been shot down three days earlier. The 2nd Lt. looked stunned for a moment and then said: "Twenty-five crews left the States together. Sixteen of us got here together". Makowski had not been in our Squadron long enough for us to more than recognize the name from the poop sheet. The Lieutenant very sadly continued: "Not even half of us are still here together after less than a month."

Our C.O., Captain Don scheduled me for a practice mission on a radar ship. I went to see him and said that I had not done any air work in radar. He explained that I was to check out for Squadron Navigator. I didn't want to be Squadron Navigator. I wanted to fly the nose turret where I could get my hands on some guns, instead of being just an innocent bystander. He fairly jumped at me with elation. No one wanted to fly the nose turret with a set of maps in his lap. I don't know if it was so much more dangerous, there was almost as much protection, but there certainly was a lot more visibility. Much more flak and fighters could be seen.

That sort of surprised me. I had told Paul all along that I wanted to fly the nose turret. Evidently he had kept it a secret. So we went on a practice mission and I told the pilot when to straighten out on course and such like. We bombed the isle of Pianosa in the Adriatic. That was the regular bombing target for the 15th Air Corps. It was rumored that someone hit it once, but that was never proven. After that I was scheduled to fly nose turret. Shortly after Don had been made CO they imported a Captain Brown for Operations Officer.

With the approach of autumn we got orders to transfer our tents from one side of the road to the other and to put in a floor and walls of some sort. At first they said we would have to get firewood to keep warm but that was not available so they said we would use gas in the winter. Juan, one of the other flyers, had a pile of bricks (limestone, I believe) which we bought. He had given up the idea of building. We finagled a truck and got some barrels of lime and coarse sand.

At first Peter wanted us to do the building. I objected feeling that somebody might later relegate himself to do supervising only. But we started to lay the first row. That was enough. We contracted with a few Eye-ties to do the job. Offered them an old pair of G.I. shoes and about 2600 lira for a cement floor, four walls and a fireplace with a chimney. They were eager and did a bang-up job. The biggest problem was getting enough lumber for the roof. Some of the Ground Officers completed theirs and we had a good working model. We got a P-38 belly tank to set up for running water. But no one was eager to torch off the gasoline residue inside. For some whiskey we got enough smooth plexiglass for the three large windows. Then someone stole one pane and we had to get another.

Hearing that Jack, one of our buddies was at Lecce we went to see him. Being a radar bombardier he had really travelled in the worst weather. He had gotten in only six mission which included a lot of Ploesti. Jack had a big disadvantage of travelling continuously with different crews and pilots. His group had been training for night missions which they all hated. On a briefed night mission to France they had really gotten worried. As I recall, the first ship to take off clipped its undercarriage just past the runway and crashed. The second ship took off and started circling. The third ship took off and just blew up. The fourth ship took off and collided with the second ship. Jack said that he was in the fifth ship just praying as they lined up with the runway. Then the Operations Officer in the Tower called off the mission.

In briefing for a little town north of a large lake the bombardiers were warned to be very careful in picking up the target. It was one of two small towns. We were leading the high #2 flight. It was a thirty minute bomb run. Major Muck, #1 bombardier from Group was in the lead plane. There wasn't any flack to contend with as we settled on the bomb run southeast. Buddy was operating the sight and lined up the target. Then we waited for the lead ship to drop. As Buddy checked off the time to drop the lead plane shot off two red flares. From the poop ship that meant abandoning the original target. Buddy said that he had the right target correctly lined up and dropped our bombs. The whole Group got confused. Some dropped on the flare signal. From that point on the Group made a 360 degree turn to the right. The Major had realized at the last minute that he had lined up on the wrong target. He held his bombs. Most of the bombs were dropped out while the Group was making the turn. When we completed the 360, the lead ship and a few others who still had their bombs, dropped them. Everything considered, we must have plowed up a pretty big area for the farmers. It was rumored that no bomb got within five miles of the real target.

The first two times at Ploesti the target was pretty well covered by smudge pot smoke. Then it was a job for radar. On one of those missions we were the only ones to get back to our Squadron. The second time we were the only ones to get back to our Squadron was when the target was in Austria.

When Romania capitulated, the Air Corps went in to pick up the former prisoners around Ploesti. I was surprised at lunch when Hawkeye sat down next to me. We had been in Navigation school together. Hawkeye really had a tough time of it as a POW. The Romanian guards treated him terribly. He had been shot down about the first of June. The Officers got Red Cross parcels very infrequently and shared them with the enlisted men. The Romanian guards were not particularly interested in feeding them until their country surrendered. Then nothing was too good for them. Still, they got practically nothing until the Americans arrived. We were eating some poorly cooked beans for lunch. Hawkeye just gulped them down between short sentences exclaiming how fine and delicious they were. He and the others also had a nerve-wracking time sweating out the air raids.

End Of A Mission

These two photos snapped by Staff Sergeant Leo S. Stoutsenberg, of Washington, D. C., depict the struggle of a B-24 Liberator damaged by enemy planes while on a mission over Austria. In the top picture, the B-24 is hit on the left rudder and left wing. In the bottom photograph, flames have started to envelope the ship as the pilot attempts to bring the Liader control. It crashed a few moments later.
(MAAF P

24/SHOT UP EUROPE OCT 1944

The evening of October 6th, Paul's crew was scheduled, to fly deputy lead for Group with Captain Brown. Navigator Norm and Bombardier Buddy, with yours truly flying nose turret and the rest of our regular crew. Another Captain was to fly the lead plane for Group. We were briefed for the old "sausage factory". The reason I remember is because the whole Air Corps was supposed to hit the area and I was optimistic enough to think that we might do a good job now and put it out of the way permanently. I don't think I ever felt that eager before. Previously it was just another job to do.

We flew up north, east of the target. Thirty minutes before target time we started putting on our flak suits. But the helmets were another story. They all stuck together. After about five minutes of trying we gave up pulling on them and decided to cross the target without them. Then as we passed the target we could see a group of specks pass over the City. As it did so, a black cloud formed and then faded. We then made a big-arse U-turn to the left. By the time we got there the preceding wing was banging away. I still had not seen more than one color flak. The Goon's used different colored flak to signal their fighters and we (the others) could tell. But I only saw casualty in all that flak. Seemed like it hit us all at once, too. One explosion I heard distinctly and closed my eyes hard. But it was too late.

My nose turret was hit in a half-dozen places. Shattered

plexiglass powdered the inside of the turret. Not putting on a flak helmet had left my flash glasses on my forehead. As a result, my forehead, the bridge of my nose and my eyes were peppered with little plexiglass granules. It was very painful and my first thought was that I could not see any more. I felt awful. I called up Paul and said: "Nose turret hit. Can't see". Other such reports came quickly over the interphone. My forehead started to bleed, my eyes started to water and my nose started to run. All quite freely. I touched where it was bleeding and thought everything was blood.

Brown's oxygen hose had been torn in half. Probably the same large piece of flak was the one that went into his left wrist and made a bloody mess. Rodney administered two shots of morphine to Brown to kill the pain. He bandaged up the wrist and applied a tourniquet. A big blob of his flesh was on the pedestal between him and Paul. There was a hole in Brown's wrist the size of a quarter. He used his good right hand to hold his oxygen line up to his mouth to breath. Some of the others reported minor nicks from flak.

The plane had been pretty badly hit also. Numbers One and Four engines (the outboard ones) were out. At least one gas tank had been hit. There was a gas leak in the bomb bay. The hydraulic system was out—for controlling brakes and flaps and turrets. The electrical system was out. That meant practically no guns or instruments. Probably the pilots compass was good and possibly the air speed was working. Even if we could have fired the guns we might have exploded the ship with the gas leaking.

With Brown helpless, Paul had to fly the ship back to Vis practically by the seat of his pants. He revved up the two inboard engines way above S.O.P. and headed for friendly territory. Getting on interplane communication he called: "Big bird to little bird. Escort us". About ten minutes after we were hit Buddy was called back to the flight deck. I got on the interphone and asked him to look at my face to see how badly I was hit. It was very painful just to open my eyelids. The bleeding had pretty well stopped by then. The tearing had washed away some of the bigger pieces of plexiglass but there were still lots of rough pieces. It was painful just to move my eye-balls. Buddy took a look and said the damage did not look bad at all. I felt sort of funny and partially relieved then. It was a good half-hour before I could open my eyes to look at anything. And I kept trying to keep them open to help wash them out. I was much too scared to consider touching my eyes with my hands.

After about an hour I could keep my eyes open long enough to use them. Then I saw what I considered the prettiest sight in the sky. A P-51 plane named American Beauty with the pilot's name marked as Lt. Williams from the black P-51 Squadron in Italy. He kept that beautiful little P-51 tucked up right under our dead #4 engine. He had to throttle back quite a bit to stay with us and accompanied us almost all the way to the coast. By then I was using the maps and pointing out checkpoints as usual.

Paul asked Norm if he knew where we were exactly. He did but he had to convince Paul of it. He could already see the coastline and began looking for the Isle of Vis. As we approached the coast line, little bird left big bird to proceed alone. Nearing the island Paul contacted the tower. We were roughly at around 2500 feet altitude. The tower gave us instructions to jump. Paul told them that we could not jump and would have to land. I don't believe there was a single good chute/pack up front that was not soaked with oil, gas or hydraulic fluid. And the ones in the waist were probably in the same condition.

Paul suddenly announced that we could not go around again—he was going to have to land. He gave orders to Charlie to crank down the landing gear. Charlie went back to the bomb-bay catwalk and began his arduous crank job. The wheels came down slowly and we were not too sure they would get down before we did. I watched the front as we came down the approach. Buddy was next to Charlie in the well of the flight deck. Rodney was in his seat at the radar desk and Norm was on the other side of the turret. Paul and Brown were still in the pilots' seats.

About a third of the way on the approach Paul told Charlie to get started with cranking down the nose wheel. I was in the passageway on the flight deck and relayed the message. Charlie was still hard at work on the main landing gear. He looked a little beat for a moment so I told him to give the crank to Buddy to finish. Which he promptly did and went up front to the nose wheel. We had all assumed positions in which we were braced for the landing impact. At no more than 200 feet off the ground, Charlie climbed up to the flight deck and gave the okay on the landing gear. I yelled for him to brace himself for the landing. His left arm was all soaked. At first I thought it was sweat. It turned out to be hydraulic fluid.

We were making a pretty steep descent to maintain safe flying speed. Brown had used his right hand during the landing on the emergency flap system. However, he did not tell Paul about putting down the flaps. We knew that Paul was not going to make one of his paintbrush landings. The impact jarred us but luckily not very much. The plane stopped right in the middle of the runway. None of the tanks had more than twenty gallons of gas left. We could still smell the gas leaking out. I noticed a parachute hanging out of the waist window and asked about it. Paul had given orders for two parachute packs to be anchored to the waist gun mounts and spilled upon landing. As luck would have it, one of the chutes opened first and that steered us away from another plane that was stuck on the runway and the second chute straightened our course on the runway by a safe margin.

As usual, the crew examined the ship to find any pieces of flak left for souvenirs. Rodney took out the aerial camera for a souvenir. As the meat wagons (ambulances) drove up, Paul said he was not feeling so good. Small wonder, he was carrying a piece of flak in his right wrist, another piece of flak in his left foot and a third piece of flak had swiped away some of the flesh on his leg as it went by. He had not even mentioned being hurt. He had flown the flying boxcar all the way back from Austria to this little island in the Adriatic by the seat of his pants. He told us that when he got hit in his forearm he turned to Brown. Just before he asked Brown to take over he saw a blob of flesh on the pedestal between them which had come from Brown's wrist. So he just let it go and concentrated on flying the ship back.

Brown lay down in a stretcher. Paul did not want to but the medics told him to. I went along to make sure that my eyes were really okay. It was a rather steep ride up the hill to the hospital. Before going in we stopped to watch a B-24. It was alternately zooming and climbing and diving. It finally ran out of gas and dove into the sea. The British were in charge of the island camp. They told all the crippled planes to bail out instead of making crash or emergency landings. There was not much in the way of facilities for fixing the planes and lots of relics were laying around the airfield. The runway was not very long and lay in a valley.

The crews had a very bad habit of bailing out with too much altitude. We watched about three planes bail out. Something like five of the crew members drifted too far, landed in the drink and were unaccounted for.

The British doctor first went to work on Brown. That took over an hour while Paul was in pretty bad pain. The doctor called me next but I told him to take Paul. He said I would not take much time. He put a light in my eyes and began probing around for the pieces that were left. As he did so he conversationally confided to me: "You know, I'm not very experienced at this sort of thing". Guess how I felt. But he did do what was required and I felt much better without the sandpaper effect felt when moving my eyelids. I waited for Paul and then we went back to the hospital tent. It was about a hundred feet long and had room for about twenty beds. By the second day, Paul and Brown were on pins and needles. At least I could get up and around. We were given Red Cross bags containing soap, toothbrush and paste, razor and blades, and shaving cream etc. The second day it rained which hid the airfield all the while that a C-47 hovered above waiting to land and take us back to Italy. The rest of the crew had left with our equipment.

The Yugoslavians on the coast talked Italian. So I did not have too much trouble getting acquainted. I met a short fellow, Mike. Don't know who or where his parents were. He had a .25 Mauser which I wanted to buy. Yugoslavians had no use for money so he was not interested. But he saw two wrist watches on my arm and asked if I was willing to trade. Mike showed me how to field strip it then and there. He was not permitted inside the tent when we came back and I proudly displayed my war trophy. It had a beautifully formed handle which was slightly cracked.

Paul and Brown had ordered that I shave them. This I was very loathe to do even though they could not do it themselves. Mike invited me to the house where he was staying. His guardian turned out to be a barber and offered to cut my hair. I paused long enough to find out that he was allowed in the hospital tent. After finishing with Paul and Brown he looked at me. I had never had a barber shave my face and chin. After a little ribbing by the rest of the guys I finally let him. When no one else needed any work we each gave him a pack of cigarettes. He had used a straight razor and we gave him the shaving cream from our care packages to use. He would not take money but when we asked him what he would take for pay he did pick up a tube of tooth paste and asked for it. We got a few more tubes of toothpaste and gave them all to him. Much later we wondered, since we knew he did not know English, if he had not wanted the tubes of toothpaste or did he really mean the shaving cream.

In the evening Mike again brought me to his house. There were a few Englishmen, the barber, a middle-aged woman and an old man and last but not least a pretty girl of about eighteen. One of the Englishman was particularly interested in the girl, but to no avail. It seems the Yugoslavians were very strict about their women. He told me that the Yugo's would give him eggs any time he asked if they had them. And they did not want any money for them either. He had a nice little pistol. Was very eager to show me how it shot without going outside. I said it was not worth wasting the bullet. Bullets being hard to get he acquiesced.

With wine to keep us in good spirits we all sang together. The barber had a really beautiful voice. The only song we both knew was the Donkey Serenade and even for that he sang more of an operatic type version. I did my best to follow on the other songs. I got a Yugoslavian Army Star and promised Mike some Captain's bars for two more. He came very early the next morning but we had shipped out without seeing him.

A British MGB (Motor Gun Boat) took us aboard. Everybody went into the forward hold. I spent half my time on the bridge. There was not much navigation to the boat. In anything like rough weather the course could vary thirty degrees due to steering. The crew was not too much in love with the boat as a peacetime vessel although it looked quite trim. They had once been attacked by five Messerschmitts in line. After knocking out the first four, the fifth one got out of line and left. It had evidently seen enough.

About ten miles off the coast the boat caught fire in the engine room. With about half of the dozen patients helpless in the hold it was no joke. Everyone crowded around the fire while one of the sailors donned asbestos and went back into the engine room. Back in the hold I could smell funny gasses creeping in. I told Paul and Brown to come topside. Brown preferred to question so we left. I went back later to help the stretcher cases out but I had no desire just to stay in the hold. With the engines stopped the boat started swaying and swayed so much that at one point while I was standing in the hold I could see the water. In a short time a crash boat came from Manfredonia and took us aboard and back to land.

At the hospital in Foggia I requested an eye examination. When did I get it? Two minutes before Madelaine Carroll came around our ward asking if she could do anything for the guys. The Doc put a strong light on my eyes and said they were okay.

When I got back to the room Paul said that Miss Carroll had just left. Sure enough, she was in the next room writing letters for Curt, a P-38 pilot. Curt presented a sorry sight. Swathed in bandages from his waist up. Little slits were cut in the pile of bandages for his eyes, nose and mouth. When he walked into a room everyone else that could, would walk out. And he said he did not have B.O. Maybe they just could not take it. He went around visiting in the ward to cheer up all the other patients and he explained to all of them how lucky he was. According to Curt he had dived his P-38 through a cloud. But the plane stopped when it hit the ground. Only when he walked away he said that they could not find the plane. After a little questioning he did admit that they did find a little gasoline elbow still in one piece. He said rest of the pieces were small enough to fit into a bushel basket.

25/SHOT DOWN EUROPE OCT 1944

When I got back to the field on October 12, I insisted on having at least three more days of rest. My eyes still hurt although I did not have any trouble seeing. Even the myriad little penetrations were fast healing and disappearing. Each day, however, the C.O. asked me if I wanted to fly. At the end of the third day I finally said yes. Although that very day, Peter suggested that he and I get orders cut to spend a week in Rome. Paul still had no idea as to when he would get out of the hospital for good. The rest of the crew certainly were not eager to fly. Paul told them not to fly with any other crew until it was determined exactly what would be done with him. The fellows eagerly complied. But Buddy and I were not in any position to delay our flying. For one thing Buddy was still eager for promotion and saw that the only way he could get it was to become Squadron Bombardier and possibly go to Group. He wanted to get through sure enough, but that was just one of the chances we were taking anyway. I did not think that I could get to Rome anyway. They did not have any nose-navigators to spare and they seemed to pick our squadron a little more than the rest for the lead positions. It seemed that the other navigators were not eager to check out in the nose position either.

Back at the base I started to regather my flying equipment. The Doc had discharged me and I was again on flying status. So I did not want to be caught short of equipment at the last minute.

Paul's and my A-3 bags were just jammed full of ours and Brown's stuff. They even had put Brown's busted hose in the bags, both pieces. I had laboriously stencilled NUF on most of my stuff but I had a heck of a time finding it if it was not damaged. With the generous aid of supply I managed to scrape together full flying equipment.

Terry began to assume more and more of the running of the Squadron Navigator duties while the regular Squadron Navigator was in the hospital. He asked me which position I wanted to fly on the 16th of October in 1944. The Colonel was flying in the lead position and everyone said that he was a stickler for accuracy. If the plane was a mile off course he complained. It being the nose navigator's job to see to just that, I figured that there was no purpose in asking for trouble. So I decided that I would rather fly in the deputy lead position. As we were to lead the Air Corps that day, the lead position in the squadron would be the lead position in the Air Corps or the number one ship over the target. The deputy lead is to be ready at all times to take over in case the lead ship aborts(leaves the formation off schedule). Later when Phill was picking out his crew in the orderly room, Peter and I were sitting around watching him. He had decided to fly deputy lead position and let Telly fly the Colonel in lead position. In picking his crew he took some of his old-timers and then turned to Peter and me and asked if we wanted to fly with him.

Having already told Terry that I would fly deputy lead I agreed. Phill also took Peter and Buddy. Then Peter suggested that some of our enlisted men fly on the ship. Phill readily agreed. So Bill and one or two of the others were schedule to fly with us. But only Bill could not get off when they all complained. Peter was reinformed of what Paul had said about the crew not flying with any other pilots. I did not want any part of telling our crew when to fly or not when to fly. I felt it was a crap-shoot from the word go. Paul had suggested that they do not. I figured as long as our crew was split up it was not really critical who the enlisted men were that we flew with.

The briefing and take-off were routine. I took only a few maps and my escape kit and a heated suit for the nose-turret. When I got on the ramp by the plane, Sgt. Pat informed me that he had checked the turret and it was all right. I thanked him and noticed that I had forgotten to get an extension cord for my electric suit. Buddy found that he had a extra one and gave it to me. The departure on course was within a half-minute of the scheduled time and everything proceeded along very well until we got over the Adriatic Sea. Then while moving around in the nose Buddy came up against the emergency door handle and the nose wheel door dropped into the drink. It was not long after that when Buddy and Burg were almost freezing in the nose. I thought of aborting then but that never increases the total missions. Anyway, Phill did not want to abort, so we flew on. As soon as we climbed above 10,000 feet I regretted that I had not examined my equipment far more closely. My oxygen mask was very temperamental. I had gotten a large clasp and a small catch to hold the mask in place. It kept slipping off and bothered me.

About the middle of the mission we were about a minute early so the formation started zig-zaggin to kill a little time. We circled the target to the left and as we flew north we were able to see that the target itself was under a closed cover of clouds. We then turned right to the I.P. and adjusted our flak suits and helmets for the target run South. We were right on time as we picked up our run along the course of the river. I started to wind my guns up as we straightened out for the target. That put the two-inch glass right in front of me for protection from flak. This time I made sure that I put my glasses down over my eyes. Johnny asked me if I could see the fighter craft at one-o-clock high. I looked and saw and said so. They were our P-38's so that was okay.

My glasses started to frost up and I called to Burg and told him that my glasses were frosting up and that I would not be of much help to them in picking out the target. Also because it was undercast and that it would have to be a radar job which meant only the radar ship could do it. The bomb run was about nine minutes long. Shortly after we lined up on the target I could feel myself breaking out into a cold sweat. I was neither hot nor cold from the atmosphere, but I could just feel the sweat pouring out on my skin. I realized I needed a rest, but definitely. Although there was not anything I could do about it. Nothing to do but just sit and wait until it was over. No helping the bombardier or navigator line up the ship or keep enemy aircraft at a respectful distance.

Just sit there and wait for the flak. It was not long in coming either, and it was uncomfortably close. It was very apparent that the Goons below were lining up their sights on the lead ship. It seemed that as soon as I started to fly the nose position the Goon's smartened up. They exploded the bulk of the flak just in front of the planes so that the planes would run into the flak. Which we did. The flak started bursting all around us and we heard that old familiar sound like gravel falling on a tin roof. Our altitude then was around 23,000 feet.

Within the last minute of the target run before we dropped

our bombs the left waist gunner electrified us by yelling: "Fire in Number One". We fell out of formation and the flak followed the formation. For that much I felt relieved. The first thing to do in a Liberator is to get out before you get blown out. So we all hung on the interphone waiting for permission to go out on our own. But there was not any flame visible, just a dark stream of oil leaving #1 engine. So the statement was retracted. Then we got a hit in one of the gas tanks. The gas drained out and the propeller started wind-milling before it was feathered. That put another engine out of commission but the retarding effect of the windmilling just about cancelled the thrust of a third engine. So the total result was that we had the effective thrust of one engine left to keep us flying. I did not know about the second and third engines then. All I could see was that we were losing altitude and rather rapidly too. From the target time of 12:00 at 22,000 we had lost 10,000 feet in twenty minutes. About ten minutes off the target we were busily engaged in throwing all the loose furniture out. That included all the ammunition, flak suits, flak helmets and anything else that was removable. I asked Burg for oxygen. About the only things we saved were the parachutes and escape kits. But even then we were not particularly worried.

I was certainly hoping that we would not get the order to jump. We had gone through this much a good many times before. My personal desire was that we would have had our regular pilot, Paul with. I am still of the opinion that our original crew could have brought that ship back for a home base landing. There is nothing like know-how in a tight position like that. Many bomber crew members have the same faith in their regular pilot and it seemed to be the run of the mill that split crews did not come back as much as regular crews. But about twenty-five minutes after target time, Phill gave the order to jump. And Tommy and Buddy were gone. I had just gotten out of the turret about this time and the first feeling I had when I saw Buddy go was that I wished he had waited so that we would land closer together. Buddy was an old Army man and I figured he would have some very good ideas about what to do on the ground. Burg got his lines tangled and was a little excited as he decided to rip them off after a short struggle. I reached over to help him but he was in a big hurry to leave.

My chute and kit were on all right as I had about the most time waiting for the door to be clear. I started to climb over the open door and then I hesitated. I did not want to jump. Nope, you don't practice emergency parachute jumps. You could get killed just as easily during practice as during an emergency. I understand that only for C-47's the Army does not require parachutes. Also, if the jump is scheduled, two chutes are to be carried. After all, this was my first time. Paul had always brought the ship back and I felt very much attached to the home base right then. I was not the least bit eager to jump, a guy could get killed that way. So I got back up and stood on the ammo boxes to see if Peter was still there. I figured if he was still there I would go back on the interphone and ask him if he thought the two of us could take the ship back to the base. Anyway, another twenty minutes of flying would take us over the border into Yugoslavia and possible Partisan territory. We were denied the additional twenty minutes to about a 50/50 chance of meeting the Partisans. Peter was gone.

I figured that he was right behind the instrument panel and he should therefore have a very good idea of the condition of the ship. That was good enough for me. There was no better available authority then. Phill was still at the wheel of the plane but he had an awfully funny-looking smile on his face. I could not figure it out. So, of course, I was very puzzled—I still did not know if enough information had come over the interphone to prove that we had to jump. But anyway, the second time I got over the open nose wheel door I realized that there was no second choice. I was going out. I always figured that I would be afraid to jump when the time came and I remembered that at the time. So, like dipping an elbow into a hot bathtub I dangled my feet out the door. That did it. The slipstream immediately caught my feet and I thought of nothing else but exactly how I was going to get out according to instructions. I swung up on my left arm and right elbow on the floor next to the doorway and I kept my right hand on the ripcord all this time and then swung free to drop.

I dropped through the doorway on my back and with my eyes open I saw the tail of the ship pass directly over me, while I was still holding the rip cord handle. The instructions were that the best position to open the chest pack chute was to be on one's back and looking at the sky, preferably in such a position that the wind will catch the chute and pull it away from the face to keep the face from getting worn off instantaneously. It may have been coincidental that I was in the prescribed position. The next thing I knew, after a powerful jerk, was that I was standing upright in my parachute and my groin hurt. I had opened the chute right in the slipstream. I took my gloves off and tried to grasp the rings by the seat so that I could pull myself up to a sitting position in the harness. Went about two-thirds of the way down before I was able to do it. The first half of the way down I was facing the direction that the plane had taken. It was flying straight and level and I did not see another chute come out of it. I wondered then if Phill had jumped. He should have had enough time. Unless he was having difficulty with setting up the automatic pilot.

I tried to slip the chute to one side but it was no go. The wind seemed so much stronger than I, and I did not feel confident of not spilling all the air out, either. I felt very weak. I don't know if it was from the jerk of opening the chute into the slip stream or from going off oxygen at about 18,000 feet or the hurt from the harness. I either turned or got turned around and saw the long line of chutes which seemed to stretch for miles. I didn't count them but I noticed the relative position of the line of chutes and the terrain below. I figured that the best thing for me to do would be to try and meet up with the guys and devise some plan of getting back to the lines in two's or three's. While we were still coming down, the village in the valley was still shooting at the planes passing overhead. The explosions seemed too big to be just for parachutists. Although there were already countless tales of aircrews being shot at in parachutes.

Having nothing better to do I loosened the chest buckle on the chute harness to facilitate exit upon landing. (Much more important over water.) My apparent speed approaching the ground was very slow until I passed the summit of the surrounding mountains at about 6,000 feet. Then it was very fast. I started to brace myself for the shock of hitting the terra firma. Hoping like mad that I would hit some light branches in the trees to slow my descent. I put my hands over my face because I was directly over a forest and sort of bent my feet to absorb the shock of landing. I wasn't scratched at all but the parachute was spiked on the uppermost branches of the tree limbs halfway up the side of a mountain. I came to a full stop six feet off the ground. I still felt very weak. I swung over to the trunk of the tree which was about four feet away and finally managed to get a fair hold of it. With the other hand I then unbuckled the leg straps from the harness and the escape kit from the straps which were above my head. I felt extremely relieved when I grabbed that tree trunk with both hands and slid down. Then I found out that I still had my flak helmet on. I took it off but didn't throw it away at first. I would have liked to have gotten the parachute down from the tree. Not for souvenir purposes nor for an additional aid in returning but to eliminate a possible landmark for any Goons that might come halfway up the mountains to look for me.

I thought that I was at least that important. But I guess I wasn't. Anyway, I had the feeling of being in a Lion's den and wasn't the least bit desirous of meeting the beasts. The height of the mountains being 6,000 feet and the village being in the valley and me being in between, I figured that I had something like a four hour start if anybody came looking for me. But I walked up the side of a hill in the direction of the rest of the crew and then came back down to the chute but there was nothing additional I could do. I went back up the hill and on one knob, under a large tree that had an exposed root, I placed my heated suit, my Mae West, fur-lined overshoes and flak helmet. I was going to travel light and fast.

After I had pushed these articles out of sight I still had on civilian leather short boots, one pair of cotton stockings and one pair of woolen stockings that the Red Cross had given me two and a half years previously, winter underwear that the Army had issued to me about the same time, my forest green Officers' uniform, a green gabardine summer flying suit and the leather helmet and leather gloves with silk lining, in addition to the escape kit I had put together. The escape kit included the following items:

(One D bar, fishing tackles, matches & container, two compasses, iodine swabs, 4 sticks of gum, 2 packages of benzedrine tablets(dope for prolonging energy), band aids, sulfa powder, sulfa pills, halazone tablets (for purifying water), salt tablets, atabrine tablets (for malaria), whetstone pocket, 2 hacksaw blades (about five inches long), cloth water bag, emergency kit bag(E-6) 1+1/2x5x8, soap and dish, toothbrush, razor(one-piece Gillette), ten razor blades, comb & file, metal mirror, paper cups, pencil and pen.)

Then I proceeded back a little farther and came upon one of the crew members. We saw each other at just about the same time. I was walking up the path and Sgt. Pat was hiding in some bushes. Well, that was fine. I asked him about the rest of the crew and he said that he had not seen any of them land. I suggested we go farther back up the line of our flight in order to meet some more of the crew. But he was aghast at that idea. We might get caught. He said that the best thing to do was to follow the instructions he had been given and stand pat, hide out for a day and then start tramping back to the lines. I told him that such a course would be no good because we still had a good four hour lead before anybody that followed us could get up to the side of the mountain where we were. As long as he did not want to walk back any farther and two being fine for walking out we might just as well get started. As we neared the top of the mountain on one of the brief pauses I burned my AGO pass and a few other items that I thought might prove of benefit to the Goons.

At first Pat said "Sir" to me. But I laughed and said that this was no place for formalities. Now I don't know if we would have gotten farther by being formal instead of, as I chose, to be cooperative. Phill had broken him in to be formal. Of the two, I preferred Pat because I felt he was sincere. Pat had winter GI clothes and had his leather A-2 jacket and four pairs of socks. He had his escape kit with maps and compass and tablets and saw. But what I thought best were the 20 caramels he had instead of a D-bar.

26/TYROLEAN TOUR OR ALP!ALP!
LEOBEN, AUSTRIA OCT 1944

We took inventory of our position. We were about 110 miles from both the Switzerland border and the Italian border and about 100 miles from the Yugoslavian border. So we headed almost due South tending toward the left or east about ten degrees to Yugoslavia. We had five compasses between us. The one that we found best to use was the one from the escape kit. It was about a half-inch in diameter and a quarter inch thick. It had two phosphorescent dots on the North seeking pole. It took but a moment to level it and see it in the dark. In the daytime we could use landmarks for directions after determining the direction from the sun or compass. In the dark we had to use the compass much more than the stars because most of the time we had almost solid overcasts. My compass checked within five degrees of due North by the stars and that was plenty close enough for our usage. We hoped to get far enough into Yugoslavia to contact Partisans (Allies) and get help back to the base. We felt it was a 50-50 chance there.

We left no more than twenty-five minutes after we had hit the ground to get a good head start on any Goons pursuing us. The first thing we did was head right over the top of a mountain. The second thing we did was to find a deer path going in our direction. Maybe it was a goat path. Anyway it turned into a rabbit path and we had to crawl through the bushes on our hands and knees. And we could still pick our teeth from that morning's breakfast. Then the rabbit path ran out as we neared the mountain top. So we just crawled through and around the bushes. Then the bushes ran out and we could almost stand upright. A good many hours after starting we reached the top. We took a good look around too. As far as we could see in every direction, there were mountains. And we seemed to be as high as the rest of them. There appeared to be less than a few hundred feet difference between the tops of the mountains. Most of them were covered with snow and the wind whistled around us almost all the time. Only around noon, when we were at the tops did we get warm. Then the sun's rays coupled with our climbing made us sweat a little. Sweating was very bad because dry clothes are much better protection against cold than sweated ones. Particularly socks. I tried to change my socks every night, that is, switch, reverse the outer of the two pairs to the inner and put them next to my feet for sleeping and the next day's walking.

Back at the base, Ed had once shown me a picture of him taken during a hike on a mountain. I remarked that he had quite a large pack for the mountain. He agreed but said that his secret was to keep a steady leisurely pace that did not require much stopping or slowing up. I recalled this and kept up a steady, slow pace. Nonetheless, we halted about every ten minutes. The regular procedure resolved itself into Pat calling a halt about every ten minutes of walking and my suggesting we move on after about a minute or so of resting. Pat was an inveterate cigarette smoker and he did not choose to stop smoking just because we happened to be climbing mountains. Which resulted in his being comparatively, regularly short of breath. He had four packs to use over a very indeterminate period and I did not say that I would give him my pack so that he might use his more sparingly. Now I may not have been able to go much further without stopping myself but I did not get the opportunity to find out.

We looked down into the valley before us and spotted a truck garden. After resting a few hours waiting for darkness we descended. At the edge of the plowed ground there was an apple tree. But the apples had been cleaned off previously. A few hundred yards farther we began searching for something to eat. The garden had been pretty well cleaned of produce also. We managed to find about three fair sized heads of cabbages and about six turnips or kohlrabies. Then a dog started to bark on the far side of the valley by the farmhouses. We walked about a half-mile and then sat down to gorge ourselves. Only the cabbages and turnips did not make up too much of a complete diet. In fact, after Pat had eaten part of a cabbage head and one turnip he did not feel like eating anymore. After a few trains had passed on the other side of the valley we continued on our way. Passing the farmhouses on the right and giving them a wide berth we sought to cross the tracks and leave the valley.

That first day we burned almost all our identifying material and climbed the side of the mountain we were on. We partly slid and partly climbed down the other side of the mountain. That took us the better part of the remainder of the day. It was getting dark fast when we spied a house almost at the valley bottom. We could hear a dog barking there so we cut a little shorter across the valley floor. Then just before we ran across the bottom we spied another hut a few hundred yards away. But directly across was a slope where two ridges came together. It was a fairly gradual slope and therefore best suited for our climb to the top of the next mountain to the south. We waited and watched for a while. Then we ran across the small level valley bed, but no hue and cry followed us so we slowed up after getting behind some trees. The ascent seemed very difficult and it was not long before we were overcome by the night. We had sampled some of the snow at altitude and filled our water bags. We poured the ice and water from our bags into some paper cups we had and drank that way. After two or three times the paper cups were separated at the seams. But we saved them. When we had to relieve ourselves they came in very handy and we had to relieve ourselves that first night's stop. After a while when we had practically stopped eating we did not have to go but very seldom.

 We found a small gully and lay down in the protection of a big tree and its root. I felt so cold that I did not get but a few hours of sleep. But I tried to relax and at least rest, between shivers, that is. Shivering kept me warmer than not shivering however. I recalled when one of Admiral Byrd's men had lectured us at school and said that for their expedition they used an extension to the nostrils made of paper. The air coming out of the lungs would deposit the moisture on the paper as ice. But that ice would warm up the outside air as it came into the nose. I had no such device. So I put my handkerchief over my nose in the best Chicago gangster style. It made a lot of difference too and I used it a good many times after that. Long after the handkerchief changed from white to tattle-tale gray and then to black and I do mean black, I still used it for everything except paper. Pat did not think it necessary to follow suit. He seemed to sleep fairly well although he complained pretty much about the discomfort. It took us the better part of the day to go up that slope and we came out into a closed valley which had some good level pastureland on the bottom. It stretched about a mile in diameter. Close to the edge that we were on was a run-down log cabin. Pat was concerned about getting near it, although no smoke came out of the chimney. We got within fifty yards of some bushes when Pat said that we ought to knock off and take at least ten. We both lay down. Pat went to sleep very quickly and I got up to investigate the cabin. I did not care to be seen and detained for more than one reason. I did not know but what they would kill me if they caught me. I still carried my dog-tags and they were marked "H". Pat had said a good many times that Abe, who was from our squadron and had been shot down earlier, feared being taken prisoner because he expected to be killed or else beaten up and tortured by the Nazis. We had heard stories of German torture even then. The infantry had told us that the "Goons" did not fight clean anymore. Well, I did not hanker to get caught if I could possibly help it. I expected, at the very least, to be tortured.

But then, neither Pat nor I had ever heard of anyone walking out from this far in enemy territory. Excepting for those that could bluff their way with the language and customs or had gotten help from the subjugated peoples. It was out of the question to expect Germans or Austrians to help us because their participation in underground activities was so negligible. Also, if I got caught by myself, Pat would not only wonder what had happened but might wonder what to do next. So I reconnoitered the situation very carefully. The cabin not only turned out to be very empty but thoroughly ventilated. It had evidently been constructed a good many years ago and not been kept up. There was only a plain dirt floor and absolutely no furnishings. Some of the logs were rotting in position and others were missing.

After Pat had awakened we examined the cabin more closely but there was nothing there for us except a possible wind-break. A few hundred yards from the cabin we found a nice fresh spring. It was sunken about five feet below the surface of the valley. We drank our fill and filled our water-bags. We had to empty the snow that still had not melted. The valley had a carpet of green grass that still looked quite fresh and we found plenty of cow dung here and there, evidence of pasturing during the summer, as they appeared to be fresh. But then, there was no telling how long it would have taken to dry them out. The opposite end of the valley appeared too high and too formidable to attempt scaling it that evening. There was a little hill inside the valley on the opposite side and we passed by it going south to climb over the top and out. We slept near the base of the mountain that night for a few hours and continued up it the next morning.

On the way up we passed a few caves and slowed up to make sure that they were empty. It seemed like everyone had left the area for the winter. We got up to the top of the mountain in the afternoon. Gazing over the very edge of it we could see no path going down the other side. It looked steeper than anything we had done before and it was a long, long way down. While we were looking we saw two men in dark clothes going along the path at the bottom. At a turn in the path one of them stopped and the other continued on another hundred feet to approach a large cabin. I figured that they might possibly be some of our men because of the cautious way they approached and their dark clothing (flying suits or greens). The other must have given the go-ahead because the second one then approached the cabin and they went out of sight. We could not tell just where they went after that but there was too much chance of someone else hearing us if we yelled to them. A very loud yell would most probably have just gone on echoing and echoing amongst those hills and mountains and valleys.

The valley bottom that we were looking at seemed to start towards our left and get deeper and wider to the right. It was decided to go to the left and try to get into the valley that way. I was doing most of the breaking trail and leading and making the decisions. We had, of course, skipped the ridiculousness of military courtesies in such a situation. Nonetheless, Pat just did not seem to possess either the initiative or imagination desirable to make the necessary decisions for a successful walking out party. I had thrown away some clothes that might have kept me very warm while sleeping out in the cold and windy Alps. It was my earnest desire to travel light and fast. I just seemed to naturally take the lead because I had a much better idea of what I wanted. Pat had said that if there were only one or two Germans standing between us and liberty he would most certainly put up a fight. From that I figured that I was with a good man. And although I had not decided just what I would do, I expected to make that decision on the spot. Depending on exactly what the circumstances would be at the time.

Anyway I decided that we would go left. So we followed the top of the ridge. We had just started when it began to rain. We accelerated our pace so that we might descend to the cabin below and find shelter. We found a path and followed that. Then we saw some wagon trails and we followed them. But they seemed to run out on some high grass. So we kept in the same general direction and we found what looked like a river bed. Slipping and sliding down on the rocks and dirt we descended a couple of thousand feet. The bed then widened so that we could walk on dirt and grass. It was fairly pouring now and we had made a good many small turns in following the river. We finally stopped under the protection of a large tree.

We then gathered brushwood and twigs to make a fire and dry out our wet clothes. We had not been soaked clear to the skin but our limbs were soaked. We had a good many small twigs piled together and after quite a bit of effort I managed to get a fire. Then we gathered larger branches and some wet ones. While we were drying out we looked around. On our left was a steep rock cliff, on our right was another steep ridge and ahead of us we could see that there was no low break in the line of ridges so that we were again in a closed valley. Then we decided to retrace our steps. We had gone too far to the left in a curved line. I then told Pat that he should not be so trusting. Two heads were better than one, we were both in it together and we should do everything cooperatively. He did not have anything to say except to beef about our discomfort. His cigarettes had gotten soaked. That is, the three packs he had left; he still had one dry one and I still had one dry pack left.

It was a good deal more difficult climbing up the bed of the river than sliding down. Most of the rocks were covered with water draining from the vicinity. When we managed to climb up the ridge out of the second closed valley it was beginning to get dark. We tried to retrace our steps and find the cabin in the first closed valley. But we had unknowingly gone much too far to the left. We could not see the cabin nor place it exactly. Instead, we had played hop-scotch with two branches of a river which made a straight course difficult and confusing.

Finally, I acceded to Pat's complaints and we bedded down. I tried over a dozen times to start a fire with my cigarette lighter. Pat finally got tired of watching and said to give it up. Sure he wanted a fire but he did not think that I could light one. Nor did he want to try. Pat dropped off to sleep. Finally I got it lit. Then I had to stay awake to keep it fed with dry sticks. Pat would not keep up the fire by himself. I finally let it go out and tried to sleep.

Upon waking up the next morning we found that we had slept about a mile from the cabin we had wanted the night before. We went back up the mountainside to exactly the same place we had been the day before. But there was a world of difference today. Today, I stuck my head over the top and fifty feet below were tracks made by deer. How did I recognize the tracks as deer? There were a half dozen small deer gamboling on the side of the mountain.

Parts of this mountainside were all so steep that they were hidden from view at the top. We sat down gingerly at the summit and in a seated position we slowly edged down the first fifty feet. We could just carefully walk in the deer tracks. Only they ran off to the sides and after an hour we had to leave the tracks. By the time we were halfway down, the stillness and quiet seemed to indicate that the valley was at present uninhabited. Then we were not too careful about knocking down the multitudinous loose stones which started small avalanches clattering for hundreds of feet and sometimes all the way to the bottom of the valley. We were sure tired of sliding and slipping when we finally did get down. There was a creek running through the valley and as we rested we took off our shoes and socks and washed our feet. The water was so cold that we could not stand immersing our feet or hands for more than a few seconds.

We used our handkerchiefs for towels.

Near the end of the valley shortly after dusk we came upon another cabin. On one side of a creek bed was a mound. In the dusk I was sure it was a hut but Pat said no. As we cautiously approached it, it turned out to be a pile of dirt. On the other side of the creek bed was a barn and a little hut. We crossed to the hidden side of the barn and entered. I wanted to go to the house but Pat vetoed that. He was positive that someone was in it. We covered ourselves up in the hay and dozed off. Early in the morning we examined the hut. It was locked and barred. The lock was very bulky. I found some wire the size of hanger wire and bent it with my pliers. With just a little maneuvering I opened the lock. Inside the first small room was a little metal stove with a pile of cordwood and a table. Inside the other small room was a built-in wooden bed with some straw bedding and also a bench. Not a single trace of food.

We had not touched any food the first day. The second day we took a square of the D-bar and repeated that the third day. Then we thought we ought to save the last two squares for an emergency. We each ate the gum and caramels at the rate of about three a day. Following a road we came back to civilization. There was a land-locked lake with a farm complete with live cow and tinkling bell on one side. On the other side we were near a woodchopper's home. We watched as four wood-choppers left, armed with axes and saws. Carefully approaching a corner of the house where we could not be seen, Pat suddenly pressed his face against the window. What do you think he saw? Another face looking out. Since it was just a kid of about fifteen we went around to the front door. He was from the Ukraine and did not speak English or Italian. I did not speak Ukrainian. He used broken German and I used chopped Yiddish. But we still had our hands and used them to good advantage. What a conversation. I knew about six words in Yiddish. He showed us our exact position on the map. He advised us to keep away from the Germans. I told him not to tell the Germans about us. He said that if he admitted talking to Amerikanisher flyers he would be kaput, meanwhile drawing his index finger across his throat from ear to ear. I was not sure if he meant he would get his throat slit or be hung by kaput. All he could spare from the woodchoppers' rations were two potatoes (not Idaho) and two carrots. Carrots, you know, improve night vision. He was sick and could not chop wood. I said "Gott su dankin" and we left.

The rest of that day was spent climbing up a mountainside out of the valley. There was a strong wind whistling across the top. On the other side were railroad tracks leading Southeast. Trains passed by every twenty five minutes or so. Spasmodic thunderclaps continuously rolled and echoed across the mountains. We were sure they sounded like the Big Guns.

We were within earshot of the front. How wonderful. In spite of knowing that the lines could not have advanced north a hundred miles in two days from where it was in Italy. We lay down and Pat went to sleep. I got up to examine our vicinity more closely. The whole side of the next mountain was all lit up with tiny electric lights.

The next morning we found out that the noises and lights came from blasting ore near Eisnerz. There was a tremendous slag pile over fifteen stories high. We went as far as we could parallel to the Railroad but we ran out of mountain top while it was still light. So we rested and killed a couple of hours still in view of Eisnerz on the other side of the valley. I was not worried about lighting fires because it would take anyone a couple of hours to get to us.

At nightfall we went about a mile to the left near a farmhouse to eliminate some steep climbing, then we came back to the right, within fifty feet of a church. There was a light in a window of the church near us. We had to pass the church in order to cross to the next mountain. Then a dog barked back at the farmhouse we had just passed. That meant we could not go back. Meanwhile, Pat balked. Said he did not want to go past the church. Said he was very concerned. Well, we did not have either too much time or much choice. I just point blank asked him whether he considered this a necessary risk or not and did he have any other ideas on how to get where we wanted to go. So reluctantly, pushing aside his misgivings he followed and we silently passed the church.

We followed a divide up the next mountain. Along the west side of the valley we followed a crushed gravel road. There was evidence of a lot of activity in the valley, but it was at rest for the night. Pat's GI shoes had rubber heels and he could put them down just a little more quietly than my leather heels. As quietly as we put our feet down it was still audible in the dark stillness of the night. At first Pat did not seem so conscious or so desirous of proceeding as inconspicuously as we possibly could. As a result I kept telling him how to walk etc. and every time he made a wrong move and kicked stones or stumbled I told him to be more careful. After a few days of this our tempers were on the ragged edge. He was then barking back at me for the same things. They could not always be helped either. By then I felt that he was as careful as possible and I stopped what had begun to resemble nagging. He followed suit and stopped criticizing me. And our tempers improved .

We passed through a little settlement and then by a sentry's hut, which latter was empty. There was a curve of about a hundred yards in the road turning to the left. Then the road turned to the right. On the right side of the road was the mountainside. On the left side was a valley with some sort of incompleted construction, part of which seemed to be underground. Where the road curved to the right, on the left side was a pile of dirt six feet high. Also on the left, a hundred feet farther was a small white barracks-like building. As we approached the middle of the turns we heard footsteps following us. Spotting the mound of dirt forty feet from the road, we hurried behind it. The footsteps approached us, then a minute later we could see a Goon walk by, just a moving mass in the darkness.

Evidently he figured that we had overheard him much later than we actually had. For he walked up to the white building and began peering into darkness around there. After about five minutes of searching he walked back down the road. I checked my watch and figured we would wait thirty minutes and then move on. Pat and I were huddled up against the dirt so as not to give a possible individual silhouette. He kept dozing off. I was very much concerned that he might snore at any moment and reminded him, although he did not snore regularly.

In twenty minutes, about thirty feet from the road and us, the Goon reappeared. Climbing up a wooden structure and facing our way he had a lighted flashlight in his hands pointed right where we were. It was so quiet then that we probably could have heard a pin drop on a carpet. Our faces hugged the dirt right then. The flashlight was not particularly strong. When he climbed up the ladder he turned the flashlight and walked to the road. Near the building he turned the light up the mountain on the right side of the road. Five minutes later we could not see nor hear him and figured that he was gone. Checking my watch, I again expected a half hour of waiting. Pat seemed to be resting well.

In twenty more minutes the Goon guard reappeared up the same ladder and repeated pretty much the same search. This time I watched him go back down the road. Again I checked my watch to wait a third half hour in the cold. At the end of that half hour the Goon had not reappeared. Rousing Pat we continued up the road. Another mile or two we heard faint voices and saw what appeared to be a building for sentries right next to the road. Then we cut off to the right, up the side of the mountain and after a half hour of slow and quiet climbing we lay down to sleep about twenty feet apart choosing suitable ground contour.

The next morning we crossed a very steep furrowed plot and we stopped long enough to cut a head of cabbage with my little scout knife. Then smoothing over the ground in the dark to make it less conspicuous we continued step by step. We continued on the west side of the mountain till we got around to its south side. By then it was too dark to continue so we bedded down again.

By dawn we awoke and built a fire. Dried our socks and huddled close to get the chill out of our bodies. I let Pat use the leather gloves and leather helmet in the daytime. But I insisted that I have them at night when we slept. Then I let him use the inner rayon gloves. I dozed fitfully and dropped one of the gloves. I felt for it but could not locate it in the stygian darkness. After a couple of hours and an hour before dawn I gave up trying to sleep. A fire was out of the question. After almost a microscopic fifteen minute search I found the glove. Then I started to look for Pat. He was nowhere to be found. I took a good look at the spot I had slept on so that I would not leave it. Then I looked over the area and still could not find Pat. Finally when dawn crept up on us I spotted Pat. Still sleeping like a baby, twenty feet from where I had slept. It was so dark that I could not distinguish him from the clumps and bushes.

We climbed over the mountainside, passing two small gauge railroads used for hauling lumber. Right after sunup the men began working so we had to watch ourselves and not make too much noise. My cloth water bag had sprung a leak and kept up a steady dripping while suspended from the E-6 bag which I kept hung around my neck. This tended to increase the freezing effect of the wind. So I had not filled my water bag. By noon, Pat had drained the last drop in his and we had not passed either a creek or snow. I told him to be patient but he was in no mood for it. He was thirsty and kept reminding me. So we edged down the mountainside keeping a lookout for small river beds. By late afternoon we had passed two dried up creeks and had come cross a small mountain stream that had little more than a trickle of water. At one spot the streams ran over a log and we pressed a paper cup to it. First we filled a bag and then dissolved a halazone tablet in it. Then Pat hurriedly gulped it down.

He then insisted that I fill my water bag even if he had to carry it. So we both carried it after that. His leather jacket did not cool off like my clothes. It is quite possible that his being so thirsty just took my mind off any possible thirst that I had. Anyway, I was no more thirsty than usual when you just feel like having a drink and you are not near a water fountain.

At dusk we again followed a road going in the general direction south. We passed through one town in the dark that had some pretty ancient stone homes. A river ran through the center of town and we kept on the road next to it. On the far side of the river a few trains passed by. Pat insisted on stopping for a while to rest. He lay down on the sidewalk and dozed off. I looked around but the inhabitants were firmly folded in the arms of Morpheus.

In the next town we passed a lighted building. There was a big sign only it was written in some "furrin" language so we could not decipher it. A few blocks farther on Pat just had to have a cigarette. No two ways about it. So we found the nearest open hallway and went in. Pat had hardly lit his cigarette when we heard the people on the second floor stirring about. We kept real quiet and the people upstairs stopped making noise. We took out the map and tried to locate our position by the glow of the cigarette while Pat took a few hard puffs. I could almost see the names but after a half dozen tries, the cigarette and we gave up.

A few more blocks and we heard the clattering of hob nails on the rough brick street. Someone was approaching and pretty fast. We were walking right in the middle of the road and could see a lantern swinging from side to side little more than a block away. On our right were stone buildings and on our left was a high fence. Pat scrambled over next to the fence and stretched out burying his face in the narrow strip of dirt between the fence and the street. I was so close behind him that I buried my face in the back of his knees. Neither of us daring to move farther apart and possibly call attention to ourselves. The watchman continued clattering down the road still swinging his lantern from side to side. I nervously kept time with the rhythm of his steps to know if he spotted us and broke step. But his cadence stayed the same as he came abreast and passed us. After he had gone on a few more blocks we got up, took a few deep breaths and were almost as good as new.

The road continued on to a lighted railroad yard which it ran through. We spotted a few people in the yard. It was pretty small so we did not want to crowd it. Instead we went to the left up a hillside that turned out to be a mountain. We had to cross a truck garden. I preferred to go around the edges and not leave noticeable tracks. But Pat could not see what the purpose in that was and walked right across the tilled soil.

We continued up the mountains when it started to rain. We stopped at another truck garden to find a cabbage head. A dog started barking. With that we felt that we were not welcome and left. The mountain grew steeper and wetter. A handrailing or fence right next to the road came in very handily to pull ourselves up. Somewhere near the top we left the railing and found some young trees with foliage and exhaustedly lay down to sleep.

The next day about noon we stopped for a short rest and I decided to shave. Pat had only a little fuzz although he was twenty-two and married. I had a real beard and it made me look pretty ferocious. I guess I hung up the mirror on a bush about five feet above the road. With a little help from Pat in pouring water and my razor and soap I managed to remove my beard.

Again to the South we had to pass through an inhabited valley. We looked around for the best way to descend but halfway down we were stuck for a while in a large barren spot. To our left in the valley was a barbed wire fenced enclosure. There were others to the right but farther away. From these others came dark uniformed groups marching along the roads. They were probably work corps as they did not seem to be armed. Although considering the distance it was hard to tell.

As soon as it got dark we crossed the barren spot. I had estimated that it would take us about two hours to get to the other side of the valley. Well, the barren spot had loose stones and was quite steep. That however, did not take too long. We got to a grove of pine trees that averaged a foot thick and spaced about twelve feet apart. The only possible way we could get down without setting too many stones clattering down was slow and laborious. We sat down and used our hands and feet. That gave us five points of contact. We did not move but one at a time. We not only had to be careful of loose stones on the steep slope, we had to see that we did not lose our hold and slide or fall, ourselves. Every time we loosened a noisy stone we waited with baited breath for a minute or so before continuing.

The enclosed camp to our left had its search-lights on to light up the perimeter to foil escape of the inmates. The light from the camp came through the trees and illuminated a good part of our way. It also silhouetted Pat and me but there was not anyone looking for us where we were. There were sounds of gay activity on our right.

After a few hours we finally got to the bottom by a tilled plot of ground. About 150 feet to our right was a house devoid of any noticeable activity. We passed by that and came upon a road. A watchman with his lantern had followed the road coming toward us and then off to the left. He disappeared in some building and we followed the road. Half an hour later we heard a watchman coming toward us following the same previous path.

We hurriedly climbed up off the road on the right side and watched him pass.

It was so dark as we walked along the valley road that we held hands so we would not get separated. Our soft footfalls seemed to echo back from the sides of the valley. Any activity in the farmhouses that lined the tops of the sides was just as noticeable. The slope came down from the right to the left and there seemed to be a river to our left. But there was no sound of running water.

The street turned off to the right and we cautiously followed it. We had gone only a couple of blocks when we heard a motor vehicle speeding toward us from the rear. We ran to the nearest large doorway and each picked a corner to make like an ostrich. The motorcycle and sidecar echoed past us. We followed it across a bridge and followed the road south on the west side of the river.

As we followed the road the neighborhood became more and more inhabited. We were on the left side of the cobblestone road while immediately on the right was a little scattering of buildings. Past those building on our right was what appeared to be a truck depot. It was next to the road and well lit up. It was too far to even cast feeble rays to where we were. Farther off to the left were more buildings or residences. Suddenly one of the doors to a building on our right swung open illuminating part of the road. We hit the dirt almost before the light got to us. Again Pat beat me at sticking our noses in the dirt. There was nothing slow about him once he put his heart and soul into it.

It turned out to be a girl leaving what we figured was a headquarters building. The hour was 21:00 Castellucia, Italy time. After she went off to our left rear we heard her footsteps die away. We got up and started to walk. That was enough. The door again clattered open and again we measured our lengths on the ground. This time the Goon came so close that I'd bet I could have touched him. But he probably would not have given us what we wanted. He passed us by out of hearing. Pat turned to me and whispered very hoarsely and with much feeling: "Please, Nick, do me a favor. Let's go back and around". Well, I certainly had no objection to that so I told him to lead the way.

We then went off to the left skirting a few houses. Back of these was a small road leading almost in the same direction as the one we had just left. After following this for an hour I told Pat that we should get back to the other road. Now descending was a problem. The little incline was no longer so little. We again resorted to the five-point sitting/moving system. This time it only took us about an hour.

It was still pitch dark as we finally stepped onto the road. There were what appeared to be a number of railroad tracks in the depression running on the other side and next to the road. By this time it was raining none too lightly and the ground and road were all wet. We had not taken but a couple of steps on the road when we heard someone coming up the steps from the railroad tracks. Without a word we sat down on our haunches, by the same edge of the road as were the tracks. Hardly daring to take a breath for fear of being overheard. We hid our faces in our arms. It was not very comfortable either. The Goon walked around us and we could hear his footsteps searching the area. He passed within a few feet of us a couple of times and then we could not tell where he was.

After a while I did not know if I was hearing footsteps or not amongst the raindrops. Finally Pat broke the waiting and suggested that we go. Since nothing happened then, we left. Another mile on we heard footsteps and took a short break off the road. It had stopped raining by then. We heard two men pass us and then we continued on into the night and morning.

I thought Pat's suggestion that we find barns to sleep in was very good. He was going to find us a fine, nice, big, comfortable barn. We kept our eyes peeled now as we passed and noticed each barn. As dawn approached, I felt that we ought to pick a barn soon, meanwhile Pat was getting tired and saying any barn I picked would be fine.

We finally climbed up off the road and made our way to a medium or small sized barn. There we managed to climb up a rough ladder into the hayloft. We could not see anything in the hay loft and just felt our way into a sleeping position. In the loft there was hardly enough hay to cover ourselves as we quickly dropped off to sleep. But it was still too cold to sleep comfortably.

We spent the whole day there. Sometime in the morning we heard chickens stirring below us. Once in a while a chicken would come upstairs, see us and start clucking very excitedly. I asked Pat if he would eat part of the chicken raw if I caught one and killed it. He said that he did not like the idea at all. Before the war, why he hardly ever ate any kind of fowl. Even in the Army he was not at all tempted to touch it. So he was not sure that he would have any.

We did not catch any chickens anyway. But in the corner of the barn, on the pile of hay that led up into the loft were laid two beautiful fresh eggs. It was not in the same corner that we relieved ourselves either. I gave one to Pat and showed him how to poke a hole in each end and suck out the contents. He had never eaten a raw egg before. Although he knew enough to tell me that the output of hens is almost constant enough to be figured and that if too many were missing the owners would know. That, incidentally, was the most delicious raw egg I have ever had the pleasure of consuming. Even Pat admitted that it tasted swell.

When it got dark, I got ready to move on and told Pat to do the same. But no, he was not moving. His feet were in much too terrible a condition. He could hardly get his shoes back on over the swollen flesh. I did not seem to realize that my feet were freezing and swelling. I do not believe the thought ever occurred to me. I felt that my shoes were harder to get on because I was getting weaker and possibly the shoe leather was shrinking. I had massaged and kneaded, but not rubbed, my feet to make them feel better. I had stepped into a cold puddle with my right foot that was covered with ice and almost invisible in the dark; so my right foot felt even more frozen than my left.

I was a little upset that Pat had waited until I was all ready before telling me that he was not going. But that was all there was to it. I told him to massage his feet all day if necessary. We were not getting any place spending our nights in the barn. We were racing our strength against time. We consumed a few of our medium sized turnips in the two days in the barn. There was nothing to do but wait around and try to rest up. Though I fretted to be up and away. The family that lived there came in the barn a few times but I could not understand what they said. Their little pooch dog did not deign to come upstairs to visit us. For which we thanked him or her, as the case might be.

I don't know if Pat felt any better the second night, but we left. We did not stick to the road too much then. I wanted a fire before we stopped to sleep again. By this time my lighter was empty of fluid. More than half of my matches were gone. I had used the lighter for Pat's cigarettes as well as all our fires. While Pat used all his matches for his cigarettes. He was down to his last pack which still had not completely dried up from the previous smoking. After it got too dark to see and we could no longer feel our way we stopped to rest for a while.

By dawn we had negotiated most of the way up the side of the mountain. On its south side amongst a grove of trees, I built a fire. As I gathered up the pieces of dead branches I started humming snatches of songs. Pat looked at me, startled and incredulously inquired: "Are you enjoying this journey?" I would have laughed then only he was too serious. So I told him that the trip was tagged with the same price whether we went through the motions of enjoying it or not. Just think, now he could say that he had hiked in the mountains in the Alps. After all, there were not so many Americans that had such an opportunity. He looked at me, still deadly serious and said: "If anyone ever mentions hiking in the Alps to me, I'll commit murder".

Since the valley to the south had plenty of activity we had to wait before we could descend. So we fiddled around and tried to get a little farther by walking to the west. Our course lay along Bruck, Graz and Maribor. Avoiding each of these spots, of course.

We followed a road going roughly west on the south side of the mountain. At one rise we saw a woman grazing some cattle. She did not see us and we passed on. Then the road ran out and we kept the general direction. A mile or two farther on we came by a small chalet. Farther on was a cleft in the mountainside. From the other side of which, and more than a mile down, could be heard the activity of a half dozen wood-choppers hard at work. There was no sign of activity in the chalet. Pat went about a hundred feet back in the woods and watched while I puttered around the house.

I went around the house trying to get in. The first door I opened was to the outhouse, which was full up (no plumbing). Then I removed the lock from the storeroom. Total contents: three bottles of something dried up, some wood and one dead cat. The dead cat stunk. I put it back and put the lock back on. Then I climbed over the roof of the outhouse to the attic. Through the fastened window I could see clothes hung out to dry.

Trying to pick the front door lock a second time, I discovered that the door was locked from the inside and the key left in the lock. I made tracks back to Pat, then we both made tracks.

Pat kept complaining about how hungry he was and how much he would like to have something hot to eat. But I had not read that far into the Magicians' Manual and could not oblige him. Pat thought that we should ask an old woman (she was old, too) watching some cattle (3 cows). I told him that we might just as well go to her farmhouse because she certainly would not have any food with her.

We waited a little while until lunch time and followed her about a mile. Then we carefully walked up to a shed. I stood watch outside while Pat loaded his pockets with potatoes. Meanwhile, Miss Austria of 1925 turned the corner of her house and saw me standing suspiciously close to her potato shed. Whispering aside to Pat that we had unexpected company, I smiled a hello at her.

She looked very puzzled as we walked up to her. There was a row of about five adjoining frame houses. I asked her "Essen?" (Eat) in my best Yiddish suddenly turned Deutsche accent. The woman did not seem to want to understand me. Her husband came out and then an old woman, the missus next door, an Italian girl of about sixteen and a little boy of about ten. The woman finally decided to understand what I said and brought us a pot of soup with dumplings, a few slices of bread and two spoons. We sat down on the nearest doorstep and ate that warm soup as fast as we could. There were close to two quarts of soup in the pot. Pat was filled up before we finished and stopped. I then finished the little that was left.

The girl started to talk to me in Italian. The little boy walked slowly around the corner of the house meanwhile looking a little more anxiously at us than the others. I offered the woman two American dollars from Pat's escape kit, which she refused. Then we left, walking at a fairly rapid pace. Pat wanted to run. I did not feel like running from anybody. About a third of a mile away we turned to the right and a little down towards a large cleft in the mountainside. Another fifty feet on, at the very edge of the steep slope we lay down in a small depression. Pat still wanted to run. I just did not feel like running. I figured that if they were after us and used dogs we could not go far enough, fast enough. Without dogs, we could hide ourselves. But Pat still wanted to put more distance between us and the farmhouse. I finally consented after about five minutes and we stood up.

That was all, buster. The farmer was looking at us across a double barrelled shotgun. As soon as he saw us, he started yelling excitedly:

"Raus, raus mit der hants" (Up with the hands). I looked at him shaking with excitement and nervousness, and could not help but laugh. I just thought it was very funny. Here we were helpless. He had a loaded shotgun looking at us. And he was shaking. As I lifted my hands I told Pat to do the same. Then the farmer told us to come over. Then a local Austrian policeman started frisking us. I asked what they were looking for. He brusquely replied: "Pistola". I laughed again and said that we did not have any. That seemed to satisfy him.

Then the farmer aimed his shotgun at something and fired. There was a bang and then a sharp snap. Evidently he had hit. So again he took long and careful aim. There was a bang. Tsk, Tsk. Evidently he had missed. So I laughed another time at him. Which did not seem to make him any happier.

The farmer and the Austrian policeman then walked us back to the farmhouse and the women. The little boy was there too and I did not have to ask him where he had gone either. When the Italian girl saw us again she said: "Now you are kaput". I figured that meant we would be hung or something and started to ask her exactly what she meant only the policeman started listening to the conversation and I cut it short. If he did not have any such ideas, I certainly did not want to give him any.

I told Pat to kill time, to stall, take a drink of water, fill our water bags. Anything at all, we were not in any hurry now. But Pat was upset by our capture and was not sure about doing anything. With his pistola in his holster the policeman led us to the nearest work office in the village. We marched down the steps with a few small kids watching us from the top. I wondered to myself what Pat would do if I tripped the guard and tried to get his gun. At least we had spent nine days in the Alps before we got captured.

Name: ....

Vorname: ...

Dienstgrad:

Erk.-Marke:

Serv.-Nr.: ...

Nationalität

Baracke: 17/1

Raum: /15.

F II / 118

V. VIII. 2877 K

27/GORIOUS DEUTSCHES REICH FRANKFURT/WETZLAR, GERMANY OCT/ NOV 1944

We were marched into a work office. Outside we could see men dressed as laborers busying themselves in the yard and around a truck. I think they were shipping lumber from here. We were seated on a bench next to the manager's desk. The policeman told him what happened and the manager got busy on the phone. A member of the "partei" stuck his nose in followed by a big heavy body. This self-inflated politician asked a few brusque questions and then told the manager and policeman a few things. It appeared as if he would be aghast at any contrary thoughts in their minds. He seemed bent on looking through us in an effort to make us cower and wilt. I could not see any possible advantage in cowering so I gave him back look for look.

As soon as we sat down on the bench we looked over our stock of food. The first thing we ate were the two squares of D-bar chocolate that we had saved for an emergency. We still had one turnip left, the bunch of potatoes from the last farm and a few green apples we had picked earlier in the day. In the office was a picture of Hitler. It had evidently served as a model for the manager. He had the same mustache to a "T" and the same part in his hair. There was an unmistakeable resemblance to the rest of his features with the main exception of the cheekbones. Pat and I remarked about it to each other. I picked up a Goon newspaper from the desk to see if I could make head or tail of it. But the politician thought otherwise and grabbed it out of my hands. He did not like the idea at all that I might possibly be comfortable.

Shortly thereafter we were taken to the city jail. On the way I told Pat that other American soldiers would be judged by our actions so he should perk up his bearing and keep in step. But Pat was not interested. So I kept in step with him. With our portly guard directly behind us passed through the city streets. I noticed one civilian curiously watching us and then he took up an arrogant position right next to our line of travel. As we approached I could feel his antagonism and noticed the crazed look on his face. Marching erect and looking directly ahead I still kept an eye on him and braced myself for a possible onslaught. But the civilian just glared venomously as we passed. Evidently he had no love for der Amerikaner. On the way the guard took out his pocket-knife and peeled the turnip and gave it to us. After the soup and the bread and chocolate we were pretty full. Nonetheless I felt that it was best to take the turnip even though we had to force it down.

The office of the jail was a fairly large room with a fireplace. There was a chubby blond fraulein who spoke some English. The chief and guard and two others started asking me questions. The girl wanted to use English but I was more curious to see how far my Yiddish would take me in German. We wound up with a mixture. I don't believe I gave them any information with one exception. I wanted to show them that they had not caught us immediately. Thus I informed them that we had been walking for nine days. But they could have easily figured it out if they did not know it already. We had to empty our pockets on the desk. Most of the stuff was returned. With the exception of the potatoes, the wrench, the piece of wire and my Master Navigation watch. Looking at the piece of wire they made motions to indicate that it would be good to pick locks with it. I gave my impression of being confused, then comprehending, then acquiescing and then shook my head and shoulders to indicate that I would never think of that use. They looked at my wristwatch and returned it. When they put my GI issue Master watch on the desk I reached over and took it back. Immediately they filled the air with cries of: "Nix. Nix. Canst Nicht". So I resignedly put the Master watch back on the desk.

Pat and I were placed in a seven by twelve foot room with two small beds, a table and a pail. Around sunset we were brought a delicious potato stew which we hungrily consumed. The barred door opened into a walled-in yard. There was nothing to do until we got sleepy except to talk. Then about bedtime, my stomach began to suffer from excessive pains, mostly gas. Evidently the berries, green apples, dumplings and soup, and partially cooked white bread, turnip and potato stew were not mixing too well in my insides after the nine day rest that they had.

The gas pain was terrible and I yelled and beat on the door to go to the washroom. I was not the least bit proud then. I did not think I could stand the pain any longer. After over half an hour of calling for the guards I decided to use the pail. Then I fell asleep. The next morning, just as a matter of routine, the guard told me to wash out the pail. After going through so much in order to keep from using it, I found out that was what it was intended to be used for.

That morning another soldier came and took us to a regular

Army P.W. Camp. It did not seem too large. Possibly a dozen or so barracks. We learned that it had not been intended for Americans. There were a few Russian prisoners as permanent personnel to keep up the camp. We were first assigned to a barracks with another P.W. He was a Franchaise. He had been a prisoner of the Goons since France had been overrun. We felt that was a terrible long time.

We told the Frenchman that France had been re-taken by the Allies. He was so deeply moved that it felt good just to watch him. That first barracks consisted mainly of a large room with a dozen benches and bunks and supporting posts and two stoves. On one of the posts we saw Shure's name written in pencil. I told Pat to inscribe our names and date below. Shure had been there a week ahead of us. With the exception of what was in our pockets the guard made us put everything in a small storeroom next to the large room.

We ate our meal in the barracks with the Frenchman and then were moved. Our new quarters consisted of a ten by ten foot room with two bunks, a bench and a stove. There were double windows, the outer ones being fastened from the outside. One of the outer panes was broken. Through the broken window we conversed with the Russians. The same as with the Frenchman, they spoke German and I spoke Yiddish and with plenty of hand motions we managed to understand each other.

They had been P.W.'s for almost four years now. They were so overjoyed to find out that the Goons were being pushed out of Russia they laughed with tears in their eyes. Then they could not do enough for us. They supplemented our rations with a few potatoes and apples almost every day. They brought tobacco and matches and papers for Pat. They gave me a bottle of fluid for my lighter.

I really welcomed those extra potatoes and apples too. I felt that I was starving. At that time I figured we were better by ourselves in the Alps. It probably was not really so but I never would have believed it then. Maybe the difference was that I was no longer breathing free air. But I sure thought that I was starving. We got about a quarter-loaf of a larger round bread a day, a big bowl of stew and coffee. Once we even got milk. We got potatoes and a few other things too. But I always felt hungry. Little did they know then. I still had my scout knife. The guard always sliced our bread. In order to keep it secret that I had my knife and was using it, we had the guard cut a few slices each time. Then as we ate we cut.

Meanwhile, without treatment, my frozen infected right big toe got worse. We could shower and shave and there was a pail in our room to be emptied regularly. But I could not get my canvas bag with all my first aid stuff in it. The discoloration of the infection spread till it covered most of the toenail. I kept bothering the guard for either my kit or a doctor. Though I really did not expect either.

A portly Officer came to visit us. He had a prominent paunch and was further puffed up by his own importance. And he looked mean. He started to ask me questions in a manner that would brook no filibustering. "Where you from?" So I told him "Chicago". At this the guard held up his hands and made like a machine gun: "Brrrrrr" but with a German accent. This was repeated in a number of instances when the question of origin came up. The Officer asked me my rank and I zipped down my flying suit to show him that I was a Second Lt. The guard's eyes popped when he saw that I had something on underneath the flying suit besides underwear. Then the Officer said: "What church do you go to that you should come over here and bomb the poor German civilians? After all we never did anything to America. You are not in this fight. Why do you come all the way over here?"

Later I kicked myself for not repeating what the guard had told me about the Germans bombing New York. Instead I answered: "Ich bin a Yuden". I repeated it about eight times before he decided to understand me. He also asked: "What base in Italy do you come from?" To which I said: "That I cannot tell". He did not like that and left saying: "We'll see, we can make you tell". Well, I did not know what they would do so I echoed: "We'll see".

When the Officer left I asked the guard if he was a Doctor. The guard said no. So I gave the guard a disgusted look and said I only want to see a Doctor, not guys like that. That night the guard took my shoes, my flying suit and then insisted on taking my greens for the night. I had my wallet and passbook, pen and pencil, comb and brush etc. in the pockets of my greens. Since he had always returned my shoes and flying suit in the morning I did not empty the pockets. The next morning however, the guard refused to return my greens. So I argued with him. I told him I would freeze with the thin flying suit. To which he would reply: "What about the women and children you bombed?" I told him: "Das is der kriege. Besides my pants and shirt were not going to help the those women and children now. Also, what about the Germans bombing London, Coventry, France and Poland?" Then he would reply: "Das is der kriege."

But to him it was not the same war when the Germans bombed and when the Germans were bombed. That was beyond his comprehension. At times I would argue so much that Pat would tell me to ease up. Sometimes the guard would get so excited that he would talk very fast in German. Then I could not follow him at all and would say: "Nix vershte'." He would repeat that "Nix vershte'" disgustedly and look at me as if I certainly could understand but did not want to. He knew I had helped bomb Europe and he had no love for me but he still did not touch me. Possibly if I had not been so arrogant he might have felt more like pushing me around. At least I thought he might. So I figured I might just as well say what I felt like saying.

I had managed to keep one of the six inch hacksaw blades and my small escape kit compass. For the latter I cut a slit in the seam of my underwear by the bottom buttonhole of the crotch and inserted the compass(which was about a half inch in diameter). I cut another small hole in the waistline seam and took a few days to work the hacksaw blade in. It seemed that I had nightmares every single night here. They were all pretty much the same. Pat and I were seated in one section of an outdoor restaurant. Some distance away I could see the rest of the crew enjoying themselves with the help of the underground. I wanted to shout to them and join them. But I could not for fear of raising an alarm. And somehow I felt that I had failed. And they were going off without us. Once it even became so vivid that I was awakened. The dreams never recurred after leaving that camp.

On October 30, in the evening, a Goon came armed with a Luger to take us to Wetzlar. Again I insisted on getting my greens and kit back. To no avail. We were given a rucksack and almost two loaves of bread and a little oleo for the two day journey. The Austrian guard said that we would get some soup on the way. In parting, I told him that if he had any sense he would take his wife and kids out of Vienna. The Goon hurried us along and tapping his gun, indicated that he would shoot us if we tried to escape. Pat did not want to so I carried the rucksack on my back. The guard exhorted us to hurry. We had to trot about a mile in order to catch the train. The guard seemed a little surprised that I could carry the rucksack and contents and keep up with him.

Once on the train I asked the guard in my broken German and so that the other passengers would hear what he meant when he said he would shoot us. He appeared very embarrassed and did not want to carry on any such conversation. We sat with the regular passengers. Whenever there was a shortage of seats the guard indicated for us to stand. He told us that he was an "Oberloitenant" but later I found out that he was an enlisted man. One of the passengers engaged me in conversation. He preferred to speak broken English. The guard professed that he did not understand any English. This fellow came from Vienna. He wanted to know whey we bombed his lovely city. After all, didn't the Americans and the English love it, didn't they come to visit in large droves before the war? I agreed with the latter. Yes, it was a nice city but right now it was busy manufacturing articles to wage war against us. There were many military targets in the city. That was all that we were after right now. After the war the tourists again would probably visit. But right now we were at war.

At one transfer of trains we got coffee from some German Red Cross girls. But still no soup. In changing trains at night there was a long wait inside the station. I had to go and told the guard. So he told me to go. Practically everyone else in the station was stretched out and sleeping. I walked out of the station while the ticket agent watched curiously. In the deserted streets I followed directions one block to the right and then in the first door. I am sure it would have been very simple to get lost but the idea just did not seem to have any attraction for me just then in that I would have stood out like a sore thumb in my uniform.

At Wetzlar the guard stopped at the ration office to cash in on our trip. From what I understood he was getting ration tickets and money for us although he had not given us a thing. Somehow I did not feel up to it and did not think it would do any good to raise a fuss over it.

It came to be November 1st. The first thing they did at the Frankfort Camp was to relieve us of the rucksack and the loaf of bread we had saved. Then we were moved into solitary confinement rooms about six feet by nine feet. There was a shattered window, a wooden bed with a "palliase" containing a handful of straw, and a stool with a water pitcher. Under the window was a radiator. For special guests they kept the rooms hot in summer and cool in winter. Here, also they took our shoes at night to keep us from thinking of leaving. The standard fare was an "ersatz" jam sandwich for breakfast, a plate of soup for lunch and an oleo sandwich for dinner. I had water with the bread, from the previous camp I had learned that I could not drink their ersatz coffee. To me it was just a laxative. Went right through; could not hold it at all. The water tasted so bad I could not help but figure that it must be the reason why wine is drunk so much with meals on the continent.

Here, when I asked to see a doctor I got results. The office was in a room at the end of the hall. On a table was a strange conglomeration of odds and ends of first aid items taken from American airmen and others supplied by the Goons. The Doc sat me down on a long table. He then took off the shoe and stocking from my right foot. Looked at the infection under the nail of the big toe. Took a pair of pliers and grabbed the nail, and pulled it off. While he took it off he looked at me very expectantly as if I were to yell or scream or something. But I did nothing. My feet hurt so bad from being frozen that all I could feel was a general pull on my leg. That was all. I could see the amazement on his face when he pulled off the nail. He remarked to the other Doctor: "Das ist a shtarker" (that is a strong person). Then he put powder on it and a bandage. After which I was shown back to my room.

To go to the latrine it was necessary to summon the hall guard who took his sweet time. There was a handle inside to turn a gadget in the hall off its stand. In falling it made a little click. When the guard got around to it he inquired what you wanted and then told you to be quick about it. There were some smudges on the latrine wall. Later I found out just how acute the paper shortage got at times.

The first interview was held in the same office that registered us. They told me to sit down as I walked in. That was fine by me. The fair-haired guard stayed in the room. The man behind the desk started out by saying: "Now we know you are a bright intelligent man so we are not going to fool around. This is just a matter of routine. We have all the information. We just have to go over a few things." And he motioned to a mimeographed sheet in front of him and a book which lay on the bible. He read out of the book "HISTORY OF 451ST B.G." things which I did not know and cared less. It started with the original C.O. long before my time. There were only two things I felt that I knew that he did not. Those were not touched upon. Now, for the life of me, I do not remember what those two things were.

He asked what my target was and I told him I did not remember. It was already two weeks ago and I had never made any attempt to remember. Did the plane have a "Gee" set? I did not know. I was nose navigator and it did not make any difference to me. He told me my target was Links. Now what part of it did we try to bomb? Well in order to answer that I would just have to have an airmap of the city. So he pointed to a large map of Germany and told me to point out the target. As luck would have it, the first city I saw and pointed to was a real small town and incorrect. There was a thing or two I might possibly have said that I should not have but the above was basically the way the interview went. At the end the guard said: "Gurnix Neu" in German and then said: "Nothing new" in English for my benefit.

The paper on the desk had the names of the crew members listed and some details after each name. I saw Phill, Buddy, Paul and Burg listed. I did not have time to check all the rest of the crew. The interrogator said that one of the men had died. He asked if Phill was a Captain because of his long experience. So I agreed. He also said that they knew about the B-29's being in Italy. Well, I did not know anything about them and said nothing vocally or facially.

Then the guide showed me back to the cell. The second time the fair-haired boy took me to a room for just the two of us. He sat me down and began his spiel. "Now I want you to think of this just as a hotel and think of me as your host. Nothing more." Then he began to fill out a sheet of paper beginning with the type of plane flown. It was less of the same gone over by the previous interrogator. At the end he asked, "Here, do you mind signing this?" Very much surprised I asked: "Does it make any difference whether I sign it or not?" "No", he replied. Immediately I answered: "Well, if you don't mind, I won't sign it." and that was all there was to it. Then I was summoned to another building. While waiting to see some important personage the Lt. in the room started telling me about the course of the war. About all he asked me was when did I think it would be over. I gave him my honest opinion of from two to six months. He then went on to tell me that if the paratroops succeeded in the lowlands it might be over that very fall. He told me a lot just as a matter of fact. I listened intently because I knew so little about it. He struck me as being the most intelligent Goon I saw. Then the civilian returned. Talked for a minute or two, said I could wash and shave and would leave soon. He also asked me who I voted for. When I said Roosevelt he said it really did not make too much difference. All the others who had asked me then tried to tell me that I had made a terrible mistake.

I was placed in another room to be shipped out. Then a few of us were moved across a fence into another compound. I was again paired off in a room with Pat. The next morning, Pat was called out for a few hours. He said that the civilian he went to see did not ask any questions at all. Just talked about the time he had spent in the U.S. He had been working for a light plane manufacturing company and wanted to talk about it. While he talked he fed Pat jelly bread and gave him cigarettes. Which was surely welcomed by Pat. He was often asking the guards for smokes.

Then I was called out and went to a room in another barracks. There a civilian fussed around trying to make sociable conversation. I did not know what to make of it. He offered me a smoke. I said I didn't but would take one for my buddy who smoked. So I pocketed one cigarette. Then the fellow moved the pack just out of my reach and offered no more. After about fifteen minutes a Goon officer walked in and got down to business. He tried to prove to me how the Allies were bombing so many civilians in wanton destruction. His logic ran thusly: Vienna is an old city. Its centers were settled first. Then came its industries on the outskirts. We now bombed the center. I politely interrupted to state that as nose navigator it was my job to help point out the target to the bombardier. And we did not aim at civilians. He then tried to change the subject.

Besides which, it was by now an old Goon trick to bomb civilians to fill the roads and hamper opposing Armies. That I knew from one of the Army Shorts in the series: "Why We Fight." So he asked me if I knew the specific dates on which the English and the Germans first bombed civilians.

Of course I did not know the specific dates and said so. So he built another complete, but I knew erroneous, argument about comparative dates. By then it was getting to be time to eat. He wound up by saying that I should not start to argue without knowing what I was talking about and first I should get all the facts like he had shown me.

Then I was brought to another civilian. He extolled the virtues of the glorious Deutches Reich for hours. I felt very weak and tired. Only once in a while would I interrupt to point out discrepancies but I was in no mood to argue. He had travelled all over the world. Had spent a number of years in the United States. To prove it he sang Carry Me Back To Old Virginny. He had a terrible voice and I was sure glad when he stopped. He said the slave laborers liked it here. In answer to my pointed questions regarding the barbed wire fences surrounding the labor forces and all the other restrictions, he said they could go if they wished.

They got two weeks vacation per year. Russian men were over here and Russian women were over there. Sometimes they got mixed and had a few babies. But the Germans did not care, they would just turn their heads.

I turned the discussion to the Walther pistol he was carrying. He took it out of its holster and removed the clip and then showed it to me. I looked it over while he explained its manufacture. Then I went back to my room for the dinner consisting of soup. Then we were taken back to the original building where they were still passing out soup. I really startled them by asking for some that they had left. They asked me if I had not already had soup. I didn't feel I should lie about it and said I had one bowl but would like some more. The guards looked at me as if they could not believe it. Then they shook their heads no. The very idea of seconds there was just unthinkable.

Our group of five was composed of an English Wing Commander (about equivalent to our Colonel), an English aerial engineer, an American paratrooper and Pat and myself. We were given some rations including mostly one sliced bread. After dividing almost everything, all of us except Pat were still very hungry. So we drew for that last slice of bread. The Wing Commander won and cut it up into four parts and split it amongst us. That helped to cement American-British relations. We were down only three weeks and already one-fourth of a thin slice of bread made so much difference. I could feel a listlessness trying to creep up on me which could only be attributed to the decrease of nutrition. As much as anything else, I had not gotten used to it.

The British aerial engineer had the position of co-pilot and engineer. They were not commissioned in the British Air Force. His base had been just a few hours travel from his home. Said his folks would know it the same day he was shot down. The paratrooper, I believe, had jumped in Belgium. Said he was damn lucky to escape. The Goons had strict orders not to take prisoners. His plane had left the rest of the flight and they landed at a wrong spot. They had been lucky enough to hide out and then get help from a Belgian farmer. He had hidden a half-dozen paratroopers in his basement. Every day he had brought them plenty of good food. Then one day a Goon walked in and the farmer was nowhere to be seen.

They were put inside boxcars. Officers in one car and enlisted men were piled in three or four others. The doors were not opened for about six days. A few loaves of bread were tossed in. One of the Officers escaped twice. The second time he was caught they told him they would shoot him if he tried it again. He did and they did. Then five enlisted men escaped. The Goons told the rest that if any more escaped, five would be shot for every one that tried. There were no more attempts after that.

When we got off at the station, night had fallen and we had quite a long walk to the camp at Wetzlar. A good part of it was uphill. The Wing Commander was about ten years older than I. The guards were about ten years older than the Wing Commander. The Wing Commander set up a pretty fast pace. I tried to keep abreast of him. The rest dragged behind. Several times the guards told us to walk slower. Before we finished they were really puffing.

On November 5, our outer layer of clothes was pretty thoroughly inspected. We had to strip completely and they tried to examine everything. They watched while I emptied my pockets. Then they examined all my clothes. I made no attempt to hide my watch or cigarette lighter. They found my scout knife and took it from the knee pocket of my flying suit. When the inspector got to my underwear he quickly found the hacksaw blade and uttered an ejaculation. While he ripped it out I looked a little surprised and then as if I suddenly remembered I remarked: "Oh, that's been there a long time", in German. He did not look any farther then, for which I was very thankful. The compass in the seam in the crotch was still intact.

We were given a Red Cross box containing socks, two pairs of underwear, pajamas, tobacco, pipe, razor and blades, toothbrush and paste, shaving brush and soap and comb. I still had the underwear, socks, shoes, razor, and three blades, soap and dish, my watch and escape kit compass that I had been shot down with. Once inside the compound we had plenty to eat. They served double Red Cross rations in addition to the Goon rations. Since almost everyone else was also hungry there was never anything left at the tables. I ate until it hurt. It just felt so wonderful to get a feeling of fullness inside my stomach even if it did not last long. There was no hurry to move on because the other camps did not eat anywhere as well.

We had Appel (roll call) before meals. Then I found that my feet were so badly frozen that I could not stand still for a minute on the cold ground. I just had to keep hopping around. I reported to the dispensary where the medics had me bathe my feet in lukewarm water twice a day. Pat however, did not go.

I gave away my tobacco and pipe and cigarettes in the Red Cross package partly to the English Aerial Engineer and partly to Pat. Pat thanked me for it although I think he was quite disappointed that I did not give him all the tobacco. He thought we had made a good try. We were standing in line at the mess hall just after Appel one day and he was discussing the Alps. Then he turned and said to me: "Well, we made a good try, didn't we, Nick?" I said: "Sure", but somehow I did not feel that we had done the absolutely best possible job. But that part was all over and there was no point in looking back upon it now.

Colonel Stock was C.O. or Senior Allied Officer of the camp. It was rumored that he was knocked down in a P-51 on his very first mission. He had chosen to remain here. We all wondered if it had happened on purpose. But of course, there was no way of finding out. He did a tremendous job of cheering up the men. Everyone left in higher spirits than when they came to the camp. There was something doing every evening. Lots of local talent came through. Everyone thought the Colonel was quite a card. He had a war resume from the new prisoners to determine the positions of the Allies. There was lots of community singing. Lt. Ladd, Camp Adjutant, served as the M.C. of a burlesque radio program. It accentuated the formation of intestinal gases of the Glorious German bread. "Are you a social outcast? Well, now you too can possess the ability to break into and break up any social affair. Become your own jet-propelled vehicle. Eat our Genuine German Issue Bread. Made of only the finest sawdust." They advertised for a typist so I got to help Lt. Ladd type up the radio scripts. I even put in a word here and there, when he was looking too.

He said there would be a very rigid inspection for all pens, pencils, lighters, etc. upon leaving this camp. So I gave him my lighter with my name and address to hold indefinitely. I did not bother to ask to remain at that camp because it was common knowledge that the staff was too large already.

They shipped out about a hundred officers together. The inspection consisted mostly of sticking knives into the soap we had to see if anything was concealed. We were issued a half parcel for the three and a half days expected train ride. We were issued bread and water on the train. Our guard got us a canteen full of beer for our compartment only. We gave him a few of our Red Cross package cigarettes. Evidently, it was not enough because the beer was not repeated. It was cool and tasted very much like American beer. Although now, I don't know why it shouldn't. Course, most everything else we tasted was ersatz. I traded one of the guards for some small grade C apples and passed them out amongst the fellows in the compartment.

There was room for six in the compartment so they put eight fellows in. We discussed a lot of things on that trip. Brook was a Theological student from N.Y. He had a 20mm shell explode in his cockpit. The explosion injured his limbs and body. The blood clotted to his clothes and in walking the sores opened up and then closed again a few times. He had hidden out for ten days. Once he had walked up to a farmer to ask for help. The farmer pulled a gun on him. He knocked the gun down and started scrambling away. He still had to limp but was lucky not to get shot. Another time he was spotted in the woods by a civilian. He moved just ten feet away and the civilian returned with a Goon soldier. They did not notice him but then he got stuck at a large river between him and France. While searching for a way to get across he was picked up.

A Captain from Texas was in the compartment. His plane had been hit and most of the crew had parachuted safely. The plane blew up and the explosion threw the navigator clear out of the plane. He came to with his hands wrapped around his chest pack. As he continued falling he buckled on the pack and then pulled the rip chord and landed safely. The Captain pointed him out later. His eyes were still very much bloodshot from the force of the explosion.

With Brook the fellows discussed The Robe, a very popular current book, which some of them had read. Then they asked some questions about the tenets of Judaism. Well, I answered all I could which was not very much. They were very interested. Surprisingly enough I came across a good many people who had no idea as to what a Jew was like. I had made no attempt to hide my heritage because I was in no way ashamed of it. More than once fellows would come up to me and say: "Are you Jewish?" and then look as if they were discovering a new species. Which only amused me. The discussion on the train got along fine until Pinky kept repeating and insisting in a very loud and bellicose manner that all Jews were loud. I tried to point out the obvious error of "All" but saw that I was getting nowhere and dropped the subject. But at the same time I felt it was very obvious to everyone that Pinky was far louder and far more obnoxious than anyone.

Since the Goons had taken our loaf of bread away when we came to Frankfort I made no attempt to save anything to enter this next camp with. Most of the others had only a few items of food left.

28\SORRY SAGAN SAGA SAGAN, GERMANY NOV/JAN 1944

Leaving the railroad station, we walked in a column. The guard still gave orders in German. We were all wondering how close to camp we were, when we passed two rusty piles of tin cans. One was almost as high as a little bungalow and the other half as large. Then we knew that we must be close to a big camp. Later we found out that there were about 6,000 American Officers and 4,000 additional Allied personnel.

We went along barbed wire for two blocks and stopped at a barracks building. Going through in two's and three's we were checked off and given a quick cursory examination. In checking off my name the Goon pronounced it in German and said: "Ach, das ist Deutsche? Yah?" To which I quickly replied: "Nix, nix Deutsche." In the examination they paid the most attention for possible objects hung between the lining of the coats. I still had my compass in the seam of my underwear in the crotch. This time they did not even come close.

Outside the building they took our pictures, two at a time. My hair was not combed at all and I sure looked a sight. Then we went into three groups for three different compounds. I tried to find out where Buddy and the rest were but without any luck. Then the middle group were short two men. No one wanted to fill in. That middle group went into the Center Compound.

Later, I found out that Buddy, Peter etc. were in the Center Compound. I ended up in the West Compound.

As we marched past the barbed wire gates it seemed as if the whole camp turned out to look at us. Gordy and Harrison were here, whom I had known in Cadets. There was a short briefing in the mess hall and jelly bread and coffee afterward. Then Jimmy and John and I were assigned to Room 15 in Block 171. There were already twelve men there.

The routine of camp life revolved pretty much around the meals. Shortly after dawn we were awakened by the Sergeants coming through the halls yelling: "Time to get your hot water." Then everyone would dress and consume their breakfast coffee with a slice of bread with jam. Then we would rush to Appel. We stood at attention only while the Goon counted our block. Then we would come back to the room and clean up and wait for lunch. That usually consisted of a slice of bread with soup or drink. If the Goons did not give us soup, as on five days of the week, we had two slices of bread with whatever we could muster. Our dinner was supposed to be our best meal. Then our bowls were about two-thirds full(small bowls) of potatoes, one and sometimes two vegetables and usually a little meat. Our evening snack consisted of a slice of bread with some oleo and drink. The most popular dish was liver pate'. Some of the fellows would not eat kohlrabies while others would not eat carrots and others would not eat cabbage. Very very few ate the Goon blood sausage. Since I was only interested in food from the viewpoint of nutrition, I did not concern myself with incidental matters like taste. The blood sausage tasted horrible. In our room it was not allowed to be fried in communal pots or pans because of the lingering odor. So I made a small pan out of a can and cooked it a few times just for myself. After that the fellows were not so quick to turn it down.

At first, in order to keep busy I helped in the kitchen. I was so eager the others must have suspected something and the kitchen got a lot of help, for a while, anyway. Nobody else would think of drinking the water that was used for boiling the potatoes in until I did. Then almost everyone wanted it. After that they did not throw the potato water away. One guy next door used to take the potato peelings and make a soup out of them. In spite of that he lost fifty pounds in that camp alone. Then I found other things to interest me. Shag and Eric were the cooks when I got there. We had a regular schedule that allocated all the few jobs in the room. For a while I got interested in that schedule. Until I realized that there was no way all the jobs could be apportioned fairly. There was just not enough work to go around for fifteen people. But it was not worth any argument and everyone was pretty well satisfied with the way things were worked out. I thought our room was managed quite a bit better than most. In some of the rooms they drew cards to divide the least little thing. It may have been fair but I thought it was carrying the idea too far, as did some others. Howard was in charge of assigning the schedules for K.P., getting the hot water and cleaning the room. Since most everything in the camp centered around staying in our rooms we got to know each other pretty well. Anything other than Appel outside the room required some initiative.

Howard had been a pilot instructor. He knew planes and automobiles thoroughly. But he discussed everything with the same tone of authority. When Howard finished high school, he and his younger brother drove an auto from their home in Detroit to California and back. Of course, this was long before the

States required drivers' licenses. When I remarked about him to Russ that he had adapted himself to the present life of being a P.W. better than anyone else, Russ asked: "Is that good.?" Russ had seen his orders to go home and all he had to do was to get back to the base. He had checked out the then General of the 12th A.F. for combat flying.

Captain Russ was the Senior Officer in the room. He had led the 12th A.F. on a number of missions. He had been on his 65th mission when he got shot down. Cass, his navigator, had told him to get the hell away from the flak which was directly in their path on the bomb run. But Russ kept going and had to make a crash landing in the Po Valley. The crew was picked up by Italian Fascisti. Cass preferred to take his chances with the Goons and here they were.

Cass was fastidious in everything he did. His pilot, Russ, swore by him as a navigator. There was no question that he was very smart but he felt he had to maintain a reputation as a sharpy, even if he came out second best materially.

Shag, who was cooking when I came to the Camp, had been stationed in Panama before the war. Volunteered for Cadets from there. Came to SAACC and confused the Officers by wearing Officers' style clothes. Till they got an order prohibiting it. He was very much interested in studying Spanish. Very few of the guys liked the salmon from the R.C. package but when he flavored it with cheese they thought he was wonderful.

Benny ate like a bird. Refused to take soup if it had worms in it. Mac said, when I first arrived, that Benny was really a west side gangster from Chicago but professed to drive an oil truck around for a front. Mac was from New England. He had just graduated from school and still remembered a good deal of his "booklarnin". He loved an arguments and wasn't fussy about which subject or which side. We often argued loud and long about the advantages of hydramatics.

Meyer was an excellent civilian auto mechanic and graduated as a navigator in the Army. He was one of the very few I ever heard state that he was not afraid of combat. He had gotten over the missions too. But one of the other fellows said the statement was a lie.

John was a very moody fellow. Thought a lot and only said a little. He sustained a very bad injury on the side of his head. It was being overgrown by hair before we left. He slept in the bunk under me.

Slim had the bunk above me. When we arrived he said that this was the first opportunity he had really had to catch up on his rest. And he certainly was going to do it. But before we left, he was getting pretty tired of doing nothing.

Morry had a very fine ear for musical tones and melodies. He always insisted that he could tell P.M. (Philip Morris) from any other cigarette. While he was reading he asked for a cigarette and was given another brand already lit. When he got down to the butt he was told the name of the brand. He immediately claimed it was not a fair test.

Eric was a nice quiet reserved fellow. He had told his wife back home to give the Red Cross a hundred bucks and intended to repeat it when he got home. He did not say much but when he got angry his whole face would get red. Fighting seemed so alien to his nature. Eric and I discussed Italy and England a lot. Just as in Mark Twain's Innocents Abroad I had found Italy to be a pretty unsanitary place. Though now they had the major excuse of the ravages of the Fascistic regime and the war. But what surprised me was the big contrast between Italian homes in the States and those in Italy. Duke took personal affront at this. Duke was writing a book on a roll of toilet paper. He let a few of the guys read parts of it. At least we had enough toilet paper and that was individually distributed. I think he lost the roll later. Duke and I did not cotton to each other.

Big Joe was Mac's pilot. He was a big strong fellow and even when they cut the R.C. rations from a full parcel to a half (before I got there) he still kept active athletically more than the rest of us.

Little Joe was a fairly quiet fellow. He had worked in a tin shop and became a pilot in the Army. He was a very good poker player. Since I didn't smoke I decided to learn to play poker for cigarettes. I did fine the first day. But I was not smart enough to hide my cards from the kibitzers (and watchers). Then the kibitzers told the other players what cards I had and when I had been bluffing and when I had not. Since they knew that I sometimes bluffed they felt obligated to call me on ever play. Also, that way the other players had a decided edge on my bluffing and with my inexperience it did not take long to start losing. I actually did not know what cards beat what cards and did not learn fast enough. Little Joe was one of the big winners and I did not care to just keep losing to him so I stopped playing.

One of the disadvantages to me of getting Red Cross parcels was that there was an abundance of cigarettes. The resultant smoke reminded me too much of that old remark which was now very apra pos about cutting one's way through the smoke with a knife.

From the fellows that had been in England, I learned some of the customs of the place. They did not measure people's weight in pounds there, but it was: "How many stones do you weigh?"

And when they referred to Picadilly Commandoes, they meant the professional party girls that inhabited the Picadilly Square. And their prices were measured not in dollars but in pounds. Ten pounds meant forty dollars and that was not hay. I had heard before that they posted notices on the airfield to the effect that all women that came to the Saturday night parties were definitely supposed to be off the field by Wednesday. I understand that they meant it too. I was also told about the black cloth diamonds that the English wore on their left sleeves. That was to show the Goons that they remembered the massacre of the escaped prisoners of war, in specific violation of the Geneva Convention. Sure the Goons obeyed the Convention rules, when it was convenient.

Our dinner meal went a long way to fill us up but it was only once a day. The Goons supplemented our half parcels from the Red Cross with vegetables and potatoes daily, soup twice a week and hamburger once a week. While everyone lost weight it was not necessarily a starvation diet. Now when we sat down we could feel our bones resting almost directly on the boards. We were given a pile of straw to fill our palliases(mattresses). When we asked how come we had so much and the others so little they just laughed. They said that in two or three days our palliases would be no thicker than theirs.

Coal was very stringently rationed for each room. I first heard of chilblains here (feet swollen from the damp cold). While the others got into the habit of sitting around the fire (when there was a fire on the cold days) I had been told by the doctor not to get near the fire with my feet. The library was always crowded on cold days. A great deal of time was spent in bed to keep warm and conserve energy.

Everyone had to be identified by someone in the prison camp for purposes of Allied Security. I told them to ask Harrison but I did not remember his name well enough to be certain. But that part was quite simple because Harrison was in the same block as I.

For entertainment and recreation there were, every so often, concerts, plays, recorded music programs, skits and burlesque radio programs, wandering minstrels that went from block to block to entertain, notebooks for diaries and a very well stocked library. For news we had the Klarion and the Stump newpapers including a comic strip of "Nita Leigh, Oomph female pilot". Then there were the Goon communiques—they took a lot of reading between the lines. The Goons never lost a city. First the Goons held the line, then they consolidated new advantageous positions. Then a city would become a valiant fighting garrison, then there would be no more mention of it. In the news room one of the fellows put up some pinup pictures of his sister. They were nice ones, too. Then someone helped himself to one of them and everything came down off the bulletin boards pending the return of the pictures. But they finally gave up expecting the pictures to be returned and reinstalled most of the news. I guess it still takes all kinds under all circumstances.

The fellows organized an orchestra, a drama club and other smaller groups for purposes of participation and entertainment. Keeping oneself occupied as well as clean and warm were some of the bigger tasks. When the thermometer got stuck below zero, the Y.M.C.A. furnished the camp with several pairs of ice skates. A cleared spot inside the perimeter of the camp was marked off. Then began the mighty task of packing dirt for the sides and filling the enclosed space with water. For the latter, each room had to furnish the water detail for about a week. Thus a person from each room contributed two buckets of water at mealtime. The bucket brigade was more than a half hour long. It seemed a gigantic task for such small tools as we employed. However, it finally was finished. Then a hockey tournament was scheduled with regular skating at other times.

The funniest thing that happened, can't say the most tragic in view of the war, was when one of the fellows made himself a D-Bar pie. A D-Bar Pie was the best, most extravagant dessert available in the Camp. The D-Bar from the Red Cross parcels was made into a chocolate pudding—one of the great luxuries of the Camp. While everyone else was sitting around the fire trying to keep warm, Mort sat down with his D-Bar pie. In sitting down on the floor, the pie fell off the plate on to the dirty coal clinkers on the floor. There was a very pregnant silence at that moment. But the silence was broken when Mort started spooning up the pie with a teaspoon and remarked: "Golly, I almost lost that." The room broke up in hysterics at that.

With our forced confinement we had a number of new things to learn. Not alone because we were prisoners but also because here so little meant so much. For instance, practically nothing was wasted. When a fellow got careless, which was very seldom, and dropped some food, as he picked it up someone would say: "Almost lost that, didn't you?" Sniping or picking up small specks of food became very popular at various stages. Scrounging (or finding anything that could be used) such things as small bits of coal that were dropped in the dirt, took up time and helped keep us warmer. In the summer, there were gardens to be taken care of, not large ones but a few square feet of earth. And mealtime depended on the hours that the room had on the community stove. Running over time was very bad for good relations. When one room boiled potatoes and did not use the water for soup, to save the time of heating water they used to pour the same water from pot to pot.

Everyone took some interest in cooking. In fact, food was discussed most. They also tried to remember recipes or to make them up. Fellows kept diaries and wrote poems in their many leisure hours. There were more than a dozen kriegie clubs. But the biggest and the most successful was the Chicago Flying Kriegies. There was always an attendance of more than fifty. Every meeting included a talk. Sgt. Mark, who was secretary, gave a talk on how he got into the Army through the Black Horse Troop in Chicago. Then a former lumberjack told of his experiences in the North Woods and how he would keep warm at night in the snow by burying himself in blankets and piling snow on top.

Another of the speakers, James was disgusted with what he called the intrigue complex of the French. He had been shot down and passed around the underground in Paris. Just when the Goons were evacuating the city and the French underground told him that he was getting out and back with the Americans, the French underground was relieved of his custody. It seemed that the Goons were content to let the French feed him as long as he stayed. But as soon as he was to be moved, the Goons took over. James was then sent to a small city jail with a lot of other G.I.'s who kept joking and making noise. It was more like a picnic than a prison. He felt that was a tribute to the Americans, that they always found humor in a situation. He rode in a bus with some Frenchmen. When the bus jerked, a Frenchman yelled for first aid because he had gotten scratched. The Goons told him to come outside and he shouldered his way out of the crowded bus. One of the Goons just put a pistol to the fellows head and pulled the trigger. That sobered the G.I.'s. Then James got separated from them and ended up in a concentration camp. He was forced to work in a factory. The underground got word out and the war plant was bombed. The next day the scaffold was full with a half-dozen slave laborers walking on air. There was another American in the camp, who preferred to stay although he got James out and into a regular P.W. camp.

Some of the shows included Zippy. He was a former theatre usher from Chicago. He gave a short pantomime that really panicked the guys. He portrayed a slightly inebriated but eager enthusiast inside a dime-a-dance hall for the first time. Zippy probably did more than anyone else, at any time, in a very humurous way, to keep up the morale of the prisoners.

We were allowed to send a few postcards home when, after some months we had a semi-permanent address. But a prisoner had to be interred much longer for his mail from home to reach him.

In spite of the threat of confiscation, almost every room saved part of their food for a Christmas blowout dinner. Then an extra 5/6ths parcel came through for the occasion. It was a special Red Cross Christmas package and included such delicacies as turkey and a number of different games. Then we drew 1/6th of a British parcel which immediately started a big discussion as to which was better. There was a terrific amount of excitement in distributing the games, pipes and other articles that came with the food.

The Goons let us have Christmas day off. That meant no morning or evening Appel. So, Christmas eve, about 16:00, we all went out to Appel. Before the Goons finished counting we could hear joyful shouting from the blocks at the start of the line. About a third of the way down we could see the cause of it. They had dressed Zippy as Santa Claus. He rode around on a flashing rickety old wagon pulled by four prancing P.W.'s and a chauffeur. It kept jostling Santa Claus and his heavy bag as it jerked back and forth from block to block. The mail had been saved for a week. The letters were bundled for each block and distributed amongst gales of cheerful laughter and yelling. I had not been there long enough to expect a letter but it sure felt good to look at the happy faces of those who had gotten letters. And Zippy's antics did a lot to make the fellows forget their troubles for a while as Santa Claus added his own bag of tricks to the bag of mail that he was passing out. Actually I subconsciously envied Zippy for his talent and his ability to elicit so much laughter from everybody in our current situation.

29/ONE HELLUVA HIKE TO SPREMBURG, GERMANY JAN 1945

We were all pretty much sitting on pins and needles after Major Morris gave us the directions for marching out. Everybody hoped that we would not march. The Russians were not very far. We knew that from the German communiques. So you can understand our excitement at the prospect of freedom just 25 kilometers away.

The camp buzzed with excitement as we prepared to retire. Sometime before midnight the fateful adjutant's call sounded and then packing really began in earnest. I made a knapsack out of my Red Cross container although it was a little large. I cut a mattress cover into strips for straps. The food on hand was pretty much thrown open to anyone who wanted to carry it. With a flurry of racing pulses we filed out of our blocks and formed a line of march. Then we waited. When we saw that we were not leaving immediately some of us scrounged around in the other barracks to see if we could pick up anything of value. Everything in the barracks at that time was theoretically discarded. However, I stumbled into one room where they had evidently had a party and helped myself to the remains of some delicious D-Bar pie. In my own block I was amazed to find the large amount of paper and books that had been thrown away. for we had such a hard time to get any supplies like that. I took an additional notebook, thinking at the time that it was too bad that such hoarding prevailed amongst those in charge but no one knew when more would be available.

Since you had to carry whatever you wanted to keep, fellows were throwing things away wholesale. I packed my three blankets but most only took one or two. I filled my pack with clothes and food till it was about two-thirds full and was quite heavy. A number of the guys quickly fashioned sleighs and banded together to pull them. Some were large and some were small but all of them were heavily loaded. After we had waited more than a half hour we finally got word that it was a premature alarm and to go back and wait for another call. Which we did. The final call came at 12:30 on the 27th of January.

Again we formed a line of march, four abreast. This time it only took a little while and we marched out the front gate into the forelager. There we each got a surprise of one Red Cross parcel. Since so many of the fellows did not expect it they had to figure out exactly what to do with it. By the end of the first mile, the roadway was strewn with sleighs, which were heavily loaded down with bedding and kitchen equipment. Some of the guys had taken the tables and just overturned them and loaded them to the hilt. Those were quickly discarded as impractical. Then the fellows began ripping open their parcels and throwing the cartons away first. Then the milk cans, then even food and cigarettes. Others picked up some of what was discarded. I did not get a chance to pick up anything but neither did I discard anything. I was pretty optimistic but I figured that if anybody could march as far as we were going, I would be right there with them. This was where my previous love of walking stood me in good stead.

All that morning we marched until we got to Frieiwaldbrau at 0900 hours. It was not much of a village and we pretty much overran the place. It was very cold outside and we took turns going into one small heated room. Ten thousand of us alternated going into that room. There was another fifty that crowded into another room which was not heated and all the rest slept outside, or busied themselves with cooking food. Our block stayed pretty much together. A good many of the guys were passing out food to the villagers. Some of them would start a can and then give it, almost full, to the nearest Goon that asked. I did not think that was so smart because we had no idea of when we would get more and we also did not know just how far we would have to go on it. Late in the afternoon we were rounded up again and started marching. I looked for Shag because I thought we might make a break together. But he was nowhere around. Everyone else from our room was there. Some of the guys had made good connections with the Polish slave laborers and were all set to wait for the Russians.

This was what was known as the "Death March" in Germany. not to be compared to the Death March run by the Japanese. By the end of the second day the effects began to show. We marched mostly at night. By way of open roads across fairly level country and touching only small villages. It was bitter cold with the temperature around 10 degrees Fahrenheit or less. The wind whipped through us and some of the guys, like James, wrapped heads and shoulders in blankets, hoodlike, open in the front. It made me recall pictures I had seen in old history books. People all wrapped up in old clothes with thick bundles of rags on their feet. Non-des-cript groups with all their worldly possessions on their backs; like ragamuffins or gypsies on the move. I could now understood part of the stories behind them. We certainly bore little resemblance to a military organization.

The second day's march was from 17:30 to 24:00 hours. After an expected stop at 16 kilometers the guards said that there was not enough room for all. That was when we started to split up. I was with a group that then marched 4 kilometers more to a dance hall plastered with swastikas. Probably 5% of the fellows passed out on their feet. At this point, most of these kept marching with one or two of the stronger ones holding them erect. The condition of the footwear was extremely bad. Some of the guys had paper soles which got soaked pretty quickly. Others used whatever strings they had to hold their shoes together and on their feet. A good many wrapped rags around their feet and shoes as protection from the bitter stinging cold.

My shoes were in very good condition. Yet, by this time I felt as if I were stepping in a bloody mass of flesh at every single step. The effects of the previous freezing were not gone and as long as I walked and the blood circulated, my feet were not too cold. But to stop and stand still would quickly slow up the circulation. I changed my socks once or twice each day. The wet socks I put in my pocket to partially dry them out. Then I would put them on, still sweaty and dirty, but even such changes I considered very beneficial.

Duke was one of those that had passed out and someone yelled to take over. So I stepped up and kept jabbering away to keep him going. At the dance hall we dropped out with most of our room. Mac and Big Joe went on. I found a few feet of clear floor space and spread out Duke's and my blankets and then tucked him in. The Paratroop Doctor set up a sick call line and was promptly swamped. My feet were bleeding slightly but I did not have the nerve to bother him when I looked at the rest of the fellows. The next day we got up and folded our blankets. By then, Duke was okay again. I offered him a prune or two from my stock but I did not care to have any conversation with him. Nobody was in a hurry to get started so we lay around for a while.

On January 30 we stopped at a pottery factory at 1400 hours. We got some bread and butter. Russ and Cass rejoined us. The pottery factory was very dusty. When we had put our packs down, I took off my overcoat. I went to the other side of the large floor and when I got back my overcoat, a 38L had been switched for a 36S. I had a bunch of stuff, particularly a little tin can with my razor and blade and some other stuff that I figured I would need if I could get separated from the main groups. Of course, the switch was made in error. Anyway, that was the official line. Nobody would offer any information about how it had happened. I was upset about it of course. A 36S did not fit me but barely. Also, I was beginning to have trouble with my left knee.

A few of the other fellows tried to make out with the slave girls that were in the vicinity, before leaving, but there were just too many risks. On the 31st we walked from 12:30 to 20:00 to get into some barns after 20 kilometers. We ran into rain, slush and then hail. We were warned not to touch the seed potatoes or those for the hogs because they were sorely needed for next years crops. The next day we stopped at Spremburg which had been a Panzer base. They had left sleds, log beds and such. There we listened to a talk against Russia by the Goon propagandists. We ate barley soup till we got stuffed. The Goons bummed cigarettes from some of the P.W.'s.

February 2 we took the train, namely 54 to a cattle car. These were the famous/infamous 40 & 8's, forty cattle or eight people. We got 4/5 of a parcel and bread and butter and paste. The guards got two cartons of cigarettes and we had a songfest far into the night. The next day when we stopped we were visited by some Red Cross girls and got some soup.

February 4 at 15:00 hours we left and got to Nuremberg, Stalag XIIIP in the early morning hours. It was still bitter cold and as we gathered at the gate we practically begged to get in, hollering and banging on the gate. A fast inspection was done in the outer lager and then we were assigned about 200 to a barracks floor in "Langwasser".

30/NUREMBURG NIGHTMARE
NUREMBURG, GERMANY JAN/APR 1945

When we woke up the next morning, the first thing we thought of was to get a better permanent setup. But it took a few days to realize that "WE HAD HAD IT" again. The first week they passed out a coal ration. After that they did not even bother. We had outdoor latrines only and could not use them after lights out. We got a tub and rotated the detail to empty it every morning. Then two officers got caught sneaking into the Sgt.'s camp and drew the detail for a week. The five foot by two foot washroom would have to be rinsed out every morning to prevent the odor from becoming too strong. Sometimes the tub would be so full that it would be impossible to lift it without spilling some of its contents. When it started to get warm in March and we began to wonder just how long we would be there; we became more careful of throwing dishwater out of the windows and watering the indoor latrine. Then Major Morris assigned Howard to put in some plumbing. So he got a trough with a pipeline outside to the tub. But then we had to have another tub inside for those who had the GI's and could not wait until morning. For one thing, sanitation was one of our big problems there. Of course, the official Goon line was that all that Americans were interested in was eating, sleeping and excreting.

We were there almost a month before they got any system of

showers for us. Even then they could not or would not take care of more than 60% of the men one day each week. Our twelve-men combines brought out the cards to see who would be the lucky ones. Some of them went more to get warm in the shower room than to keep clean. They again timed the hot water and we used one spout for two or three men. For about a month we could trade soap and cigarettes with the Russians who regulated the hot water for salt, onions, utensils and a few other miscellaneous items. As usual, the fellows that had plenty of cigarettes and soap started bidding higher than those that were short. Also, the Goons probably told the Russians and others that the Americans had plenty of cigarettes. Then they wanted exorbitant amounts for any items they had. Some Russians would sneak gadgets they had made in camp and try to sell them to the Americans for cigarettes. They had canteens of different countries, very pretty inlaid boxes for jewelry, wooden shoes, cigarette holders and such.

The camp that we were to make our home for an indefinite period of time had just been evacuated by the Eye-ties. Apparently they had no opportunity for sanitation. It was terribly dirty. Everyone was covered with bites for the first few weeks. After that it seemed that some were specially picked to be molested by the lice and other bugs that infested the barracks. We got orders to air out the blankets and straw every day. The straw was taken out of our palliasses (similar to mattresses) and left to air out for a week. If it was still there, the bugs were all supposed to be gone. The straw was very good to start fires with and consequently was not safe to be kept laying around. I thought that my palliass was infested so it was used to make fires. After things were more organized, those that had palliasses with straw donated them to those who had to sleep on the floor. Then they drew cards with those that had empty palliasses to see who would keep them. There were only enough for about a third of the men. The rest would put anything like paper etc. that they could get, under their blankets to serve as insulation to cut off drafts while they slept.

The block system was continued with our own officers still as liaison for us. We had Block 171 stick together as much as possible. Less than half of the fellows were from other ones after two weeks. Then a rather strict count was taken and we were not supposed to change barracks without authorization. After two weeks, the count in our block went from over 200 to 150. By that time we were really sweating out Red Cross parcels. We did not have much of anything left. The Goons gave us some sugar and some coffee to supplement their ration of bread, butter and soup. The daily diet here consisted of two tea-cups of thin soup, one-seventh of a loaf of bread, about one-twentieth of a pound of margarine and two potatoes. The Red Cross food that we had carried to supplement this amounted to about an ounce of meat (for the most part). There was next to no meat in the soup. That is, outside of the bugs and worms. The grains that they had used to make the soup had been stored for a very long time and had gotten wormy. The peas that they used had a bug in almost every other one. Some of the fellows just could not stomach it. So I had seconds. The Docs figured we were getting about six hundred calories per day.

We were visited by the YMCA representative and the Red Cross representative and Colonel Alfalfa submitted reports to the Goon high command. The Goon Major wept when he saw how the Air Raid Shelter had been broken up for its wood. A delousing detail and a shower detail were organized. Apparently, because of the starvation rations, a number of the fellows passed out on several occasions. Spike bent over and blacked out. One of the fellows on the top (of a three high) bunk jumped down and passed out. He regained consciousness two days later. Many stayed in the bunks to conserve energy. We were all glad when the spring canteen re-opened. The daily talk was of food first, than the war, then women. Hubba-hubba. One time Russ swore at the guards. They would catch themselves just before they spoke in English and wound up speaking German. Two fellows went over the fence in a fog. But they were beat up by the SS in a railroad yard when they were caught.

    Some fellows put up lists for buying cars, pictures, maple sugar, log books etc. presuming that the war was almost over and we would be interested in those things soon. I met Joey P. in the washroom, which was a big surprise, he had taught me how to ride my motorcycle when we both went to Hyde Park High school. He would bet fellows that he could get his father's twin ignition Nash to do sixty miles an hour in second gear. He would then go over sixty miles an hour in third and then down-shift to second at that speed to win the bet.

    The other groups probably had the permission of the Goons and would have split any sales profits with them. But we had not brought practically any utensils with us and anything we could get came in handy. In going to the showers we passed an Italian hospital contingent. We tried to have them throw the knives etc. for our cigarettes over the barbed wire; but anything intercepted by the Goon guards was kept and later traded for, again, to us Americans. But that was one of the risks. The Goons would yell like mad but outside of that they did not do anything. We also passed the potato stores and toward the end we would step smoothly out of line and quickly return with whatever we could lay our hands on.

Before they started the warm showers, only a few of the hardier souls would venture to take the outdoor showers. We had two crowns or faucets for 450 men. They would keep running at full capacity with a line of varying size all day. The first month, the water was so cold that by holding your hand under it your hand would freeze. After about a week or two there was not much lumber around the waterhouse. It took a lot of nerve to stand outside and shiver in order to wash. I only took half a bath once. I had to wash my feet more often in order to make sure that I would not have a repeat of the infection. I would get up before they blew the bugle shortly after dawn. Then there would not be but a few fellows crowding the faucets. Even washing one pair of socks was a major operation. There was also a shortage of soap and those who were lucky enough to have some hung on to it. We had no idea as to when we might possibly get some more. Sanitation was the first step toward maintaining one's health.

As soon as we got wind of the big bombardment on the Rhine, we all hung on every communique. BBC gave us less information on the exact position when the Rhine was crossed, but more factual information about the general progress. The German communiques were obliged to announce the locations of the spearheads to spike false and fantastic rumors which would disrupt the unity of the Germans. As in similar cases, when the news was excellent the camp was bare of rumors. Discussion was hot and fast, and everyone was expressing his opinion on how long it would take before the Germans collapsed or were mopped up. Of course, the biggest question was: "Would we march?" Everyone was telling everyone else hopefully: "We'll never march".

Chip proved to me how illogical it would be for the Germans to march us out, so I figured if it were illogical to march, then we would. Therefor, I had my pack all ready from previous weeks, figuring there was a slight possibility of marching from Nuremberg at the time we first arrived. We had presumably learned a great deal from the previous march from Sagan. Sometime before we left and while we were taking our daily constitutional walk I put my arms around both Russ' and Chip's shoulders and asked: "If we get the opportunity, would you two be interested in trying to walk out together?" I was very pleased that they both agreed to it.

We soon detected a marked change in the attitude of our guards. We knew that if we did march it would be because of orders from higher headquarters than the German Colonel on the post. Where they had been very exacting they were now much slower to correct us. They tried to impress us with the idea that they were doing all that they could for us. We were reasonably sure that the Goon in charge of the whole Nuremberg area was limiting what was given to us. We were told that he had no love for the Air Corps, which had brought about the destruction of his supplies and had made his job extremely difficult. Our senior officers had compiled a complete set of directions which they would insist on (and did) in the event of a march. It was very well organized so that there would be no repetition of the old accordion movement. We were separated by blocks or barracks and had a "commando" or troubleshooter to each block.

Everyone was told to see one of the staff if we intended to escape from camp so that we would not violate any of the paroles. The Senior Allied Officer had to sign a parole (oath/promise?) for practically everything that came into Camp to make sure (?) that it would not be used for purposes of escape from the Camp.

31/BALKING IN BAVARIA BAVARIAN ALPS APR 1945

About 4 April we left in the third block of the second compound in the line of march. Our first stop was to be at Neumarkt. The guards threatened to fire at the G.I.'s who were trading with civilians off the road. But they all ducked and ran back to the column. Refugees from Nuremberg were filling the road with vans and bicycles. We used panels to spell out U.S. whenever we rested to avoid "Friendly Fire". On the second stop they passed out hot potatoes, Chip got some for us. Some barracks/ blocks passed each other on the road.

We later stopped in the woods and built a fire. But the guards argued against it and we doused the fire. Things acquired in trading were used when it was possible to enhance our diet. The market value of cigarettes, coffee, tea, chocolate, bread, potatoes, onions, barley, rye, marks, blood sausage and eggs became more critical because of the activity in them. One cigarette was equal to five marks which was equal to one bread. One bread equalled 50 pfennings or half a mark, all depending on how well one could trade or bargain. I acquired a Hungarian mess kit in the trading.

We went from the front of the column to the rear of the column in three days. The Red Cross trucks turned back about a mile away from us. When we went for water and talked to some

Germans, they replied in fluent German but we were puzzled as to what they said. The guards were apparently perfectly willing to get caught. We slept at Gasthous. We got to Berching too late for parcels. The Senior Allied Officer was not sure what we should do so we moved on. We passed Plankstettin. Some of the natives said hello. We camped about one and a half miles away. Then a Goon Major ordered us back to Plankstettin to join about 200 others there. We had to sleep in barns. The former tenants returned, they apparently had the run of the countryside at this time. We slept there two nights and went out daily to trade. We felt it was better than hiding out alone in a barn to kill time. One woman showed us a letter by an American—apparently she felt it was her ticket to safety when Hitler was kaput.

I talked to some Hungarian SS at the RR station, that had just gotten back from the front. They were dead tired and did not want to answer any questions and I had plenty of questions as to conditions at the front. When one soldier very wearily waved me away I got the strongest impression that he was so tired and disgusted that he would just as soon shoot me as talk to me. So I took the hint and left. We looked at the local Hungarian hospital and talked to one of the local girls who would not sell us a map she had. The soldiers were willing to trade marks for cigarettes but that did not seem to be a good idea. Abe, a former 451st bombardier, joined us at this time.

About the ninth of April we had started sewing the two barracks bags into packs and changing from white straps into black ones that would not be seen at night. The next day we went out to trade and picked up a dozen eggs and some bread and onions. When we returned to Plankstettin we found out that this main body of over 200 had moved on 3 kilometers to Beilingreis. Abe and his friend thought it best to rejoin the main body. The other three told the landlady goodbye. Whereupon she asked us when we were going to leave. A G.I. could no longer be sure of walking down the street unnoticed. Some of the fellows had made advantageous arrangements to wait for the Americans. The villagers could claim ignorance if detected by German soldiers. Whereas an American P.O.W. would be very good insurance when the G.I.'s lines enveloped the village.

It seemed that everyone was waiting for the Americans. It was only a question of time. They all wanted the Americans to come and end the war. They did not want the Russians to come. But they still were not too sure that the Americans would not rape and pillage. Even in our position of subservience they still sought reassurance of Allied policy from us. Their pathos still appeared as much of an act as anything else even then. Particularly when they asked questions about the wonderful Americans and told us how good they had been personally and how much we all had in common.

It was no longer safe to stay in the village without some special arrangements but we did stall the landlady off another day by telling her that we would rejoin the main group on the morrow. We left our little barn about eleven o'clock in the morning. There was a pile of trash in the barn which we did not care about. We decided to give two nice white china bowls, no longer desirable for carrying, to the landlady. She was so overwhelmed, either because of our departure or the gift or both, that she gave us half a bread. I felt guilty about taking it but the feeling did not slow up my reaching for it in the slightest. After all it was for a good cause and charity still began at home for us. On leaving we kept off the main highway and took a side road to go to a village adjacent to Beilingreis.

We walked about two kilometers and parked our packs. From this position we could look into the village next to Beilingreis. After casing the countryside, Russ and I started to walk down to trade with the villagers. Just about that time the 8th and 15th Air Corps seemed to be reaching their targets for the day. Smoke bombs from the lead ships could be seen on every 15 to 20 degrees of the compass. Little children, about three to six years old, more or less, could be seen, throwing themselves down and digging their noses into the dirt alongside the road. The bigger children, like the adults, but with more excitement, counted the planes that they could see. As we walked through the town we could not help but feel that the people would be very unsympathetic with our desire to trade for food. So we took a powder. Back on the hillside, half a dozen Goon soldiers, without investigating, passed us. We had some of our blankets spread as if we were picnicking. One of the soldiers we recognized as being from Plankstettin but we did not say hello and neither did he. He seemed much more interested in the young fraulein with him. Later Chip and I went back into town but were only able to promote a few slices of bread. The absence of the other G.I.'s was rather obvious as well as a good indication that they had now gotten sufficient guards.

Putting our packs together and leaving a few more articles we kept to the woods, heading for Rudertshofen. We hid our packs in the woods and circled to come in on a south heading. As we entered the town a man with a very crafty gleam in his eye caught up with us and engaged us in conversation. This was our good friend the burgomeister. We stopped in front of the school and also talked to the schoolmaster. While the children inside excitedly crowded to the windows to see what was going on.

I had a pronounced limp in my right foot to indicate that I was not in a position to do a lot of walking. I limped on my right foot because that big toenail had been pulled off and was still a little tender, therefore I could remember it more easily. By that time it was almost easier to limp than to walk naturally. We all looked beat from walking. Our previous trading experience stood us in good stead and we were cued to the gills for the right responses. Our story was that we were trying to catch up to the main body; which was supposed to be in Birching or Plankstettin. They informed us that the last ones in Birching had gone on. We did not know that. But what was more important, they did not know that the P.O.W.'s were also supposed to have left Plankstettin the previous day. They wanted to know why we did not have a guard. To which I laughingly replied that we did not need a guard because everybody in Germany knew where we were going. That made good sense to them. They also wanted to know why we did not head for the lines. Assuming a crafty look I inquired as to our distance from the lines. The schoolteacher said it was a hundred kilometers. I was positive that he was lying. Then looking very resigned I answered that was much too far for us.

We agreed that the blankets we had (9) were too heavy for us to carry any further. We would like to trade them for food. We were very hungry. All that the Goon guards had given us was 2/3 of a cup of macaroni. Wouldn't someone please cook it for us. The schoolteacher broke the ice by having his wife give us three big slices of bread. Then the burgomeister agreed to have his wife cook the macaroni for us. We figured that they would have to add at least some potatoes and if we were lucky, some onions. Which they did. We made fast work of the stew. The wife also made us six fried eggs and pan fried potatoes. We felt very comfortable after putting that away. It was almost like learning to eat again. While we were waiting the schoolteacher came in and we gave him a cigarette. We gave the burgomeister a couple of cigarettes to smoke as we ate and four of the blankets.

Talking to the burgomeister between and during the meal he took the attitude that the German people would be very glad to see our buddies overrun the land and end the war. I told him that the German people were not so bad as much as they were being run by the Partei, the SS and the Army. Those were the ones with whom we had the quarrel. He readily agreed. We looked around the room while waiting for the macaroni to be cooked. It was a large spacious room. There was a stove with a front that appeared to be tile. The China cabinet had a score or so of beer steins in it and seemed quite ready for a village party except that they claimed that they had no beer for a very long time. There was also a bowling alley (pin ball style) and the burgomeister and his dad showed us how they played it. The dad walked around the room and talked to us a little very conspicuously waving around an empty tobacco pipe in his hand. But we did not take the hint.

Another villager came in while we were alone and started to dicker with us for the few, so he thought, remaining cigarettes. We gave him two blankets and about five cigarettes and told him what we wanted. He came back with a bag of rye, six eggs, two-thirds of a bread and two pieces of link sausage with some grease. But that deal was on the QT as he did not want the others to know about it either. The burgomeister's wife must have been told that we had the three slices of bread because she did not give us any. When we left the burgomeister's house we figured that we had gotten all the food from that town that we could as we could not proceed to barter with the other villagers without exciting new suspicions. But an ex-soldier, who had lost a leg on the Russian front waved us in to his house. He told us that the burgomeister was a plenty bad fellow, strictly a party man. Though now he was slowly swinging around. We got a big pan of sauerkraut, some good sized pieces of meat and about half a bread. We even had to slow up in order to finish it. We gave the soldier and his family a blanket and two cups which they seemed to appreciate greatly. Their house was pretty dirty and untidy on the inside. One of their children was very sick. I even hesitated about using one of the forks that was on the table, but not so that you could notice. We left town in the direction of Plankstettin and then circled back to our packs. We hard-boiled the eggs that evening, slung our packs on our backs and were off.

32/TURN AROUND WURTZBURG, AUSTRIA APR 1945

We starting climbing down what we thought was the last big mountainside. From then on we did not do very much travelling in the daytime. By mutual agreement, Chip did most of the leading. He seemed to keep a heading very well in spite of the hills, valley, rivers, woods and roads. We still checked by the compass regularly, sometimes as often as every minute, sometimes every half hour. It was still correct to within five degrees according to the stars. For us that was plenty close enough. A good part of the time we could not see good landmarks. Also, with the frequent overcasts, the compass still came in very handy. At times it was so dark that we could not see objects more than thirty to forty feet in front of us—sides and rear too.

We slept out in the open. Being very careful to choose cutover groves of pines when possible. That is, those younger trees which did not have their lower limbs trimmed. Thus, affording good cover in the foliage. We bedded down with two blankets underneath and three on top. Sometimes we cut branches for additional camouflage. Sometimes we cut pine needles for a mattress for additional comfort. We were very lucky because after leaving the column we did not experience enough rain to thoroughly soak the blankets. Although they did become quite damp a few times.

In crossing one valley in pitch dark we had to cross a fairly busy road. We travelled adjacent to the road for about four hours and could see the headlights on the cars and trucks and the lamps on the horses and wagons. We were close enough to hear the drivers yelling at the horses and the squeaking of the wheels. We finished the last of the iron rations while looking at the roads and lights.

The land seemed to be downgrade in the west and we thought it best to cross the road to the north. The road curved to the north and as we approached to cross it we had to lie down a few times while headlights illuminated the countryside around us. At first I thought we were under the beams of a searchlight because it seemed as though a sentry was challenging some of the vehicles. We then neared the road away from where we placed the sentry and listened carefully for approaching vehicles. We quickly crossed the road and then a bridge and then found an additional creek by getting our feet wet in it. I jumped as quick and as far as I could and warned Chip and Russ after getting one foot wet. They walked a little farther on trying to find a better place to cross, but then wound up with getting their feet wet. We went up the next mountainside to the edge of the woods and stretched out. I wiped my foot a little—not wanting to risk any more infection or freezing. The wind was cold and added to the drizzle, made for much discomfort. After a few hours, we decided that it was best to move on.

We walked across a big valley and up another mountainside through a forest reaching the edge of a plateau and slept. We could hear farmers and village dogs less than two miles away. We heard and saw plowing in the daytime. We refilled our water bottles. We crossed some railroad tracks near the village just before the train passed. The village dogs started barking. We waited for a crowd of men to pass and could not see any women with them after we had already waited for the activity to cease upon reaching the end of the plain.

We finally did cross the last mountainside and could see south of the Bavarian Alps to the level country ahead. But walking halfway down the mountain we suddenly came upon a German soldier facing south, fast asleep with his rifle across his feet and his back against a tree. All at once it became most critical not to make a sound. We immediately backed up and walked to the left to stay out of his sight if he awoke. Upon moving several hundred feet we again started to descend this last mountain. In the valley, Russ pointed out that something big had exploded and the blast was climbing up to the sky. I looked where he pointed and at first I could not see anything but then the rising cloud of smoke became most obvious. But we could not tell who had set it off. We saw a farmer plowing the field in the valley a couple of miles away. To our right, about a mile from the farmer there was a large grove of trees which looked like a good place to spend the night.

We descended the mountain and made for the grove of trees and spent the night in them. The next morning when we awoke we started a campfire and cooked some of the food we had. We figured that no one could see the smoke amongst the trees. The farmer again was plowing his field the next day. We thought we had best wait for the darkness of night to walk in the valley to decrease the chances of being seen. But during the day a half dozen vehicles approached going north towards the mountain. One of the others made the remark that the vehicles looked like American jeeps. But we figured that could not be right. All at once the German "88" cannon on the mountain went off and from the column of vehicles we heard: "Turn around". Chip said: "Didn't he say: 'Turn Around'?" meaning in English. We were tempted to run out then but considered it the better part of valor to wait until the darkness could cover us.

We waited until the dark of night and then took to the road leading south. The first village we came to looked extremely quiet so we went off the road and around that village. Getting back on the road we approached the next village. There we could just make out the American vehicles and G.I.'s. As we came closer a black sentry challenged us and I immediately started talking very fast to let him know that we were Americans and walking away from our German captors. He had yelled: "Halt" and then asked us to throw our dog tags to him so that he could make sure who we were. I was very happy to throw him my second (and last) dog tag which the Goons had not taken. Once it was established that we were really Americans the soldiers could not do enough for us. One of the fellows gave me his field jacket and showed us where the food was and we helped ourselves to as much as we wanted.

The next morning the soldier that had given me his field jacket asked for it back and I gave it to him. I'm sure his second thoughts revolved about him accounting for his jacket and what paper work and other trouble it would be for him to get another one. I did not mind at all returning the field jacket—it would take far, far, more to change our feeling of "Deja vu". We had our fill of breakfast and then we waited. The sentry asked several vehicle drivers if they were going back to headquarters and could they give us a lift. One driver said that he had orders to move forward and when he came back he would take us.

But he and the two other vehicles that left together towards the mountain and we never saw them come back. Another driver did give us a lift to field headquarters. I don't think that I ever saw such a large group of soldiers moving up to the front and felt so good about being amongst them. One of the soldiers pointed out a house about a mile out of town and asked if we wanted to go there. We looked at him for an explanation and he said something in French. When we looked more puzzled he translated the phrase: "Pussy for Officers." It was obviously stocked with women for the pleasure of the German Army. But we were not interested. When we got to field headquarters we got into the mess line and helped ourselves. Before we could get seconds the C.O. made some remark about how everyone was stuffing themselves and there was still a lot of fighting to do. We figured it was not worth explaining our situation to him and did not try for more.

33/PARIS IN THE SPRING PARIS, FRANCE APRIL 1945

Shortly thereafter we got a lift in a covered jeep with a small trailer. We piled our bags in the trailer and ourselves in the jeep and rode through the rain looking for division headquarters. When the traffic got really heavy, we could tell that we were approaching it. Just on the edge of camp a Colonel seemed to be directing traffic. We were all huddled in the jeep trying to keep dry under some raincoats. We were wet but certainly not miserable. As we drew up alongside the Colonel, the driver asked him where the Air Corps liaison officer was and how we could get there. Explaining that we had just reunited ourselves with the Americans. The Colonel gave us a warm welcome and said that he was very glad to have us back on his side. Russ said that he was not half as glad as we were. We found the A.C. Liaison Officer. He turned out to be a P-47 pilot who had been assigned to the infantry after doing his hundred missions. He set us up in his panel truck with a radio operator and lots of equipment. It was warm and dry and we made ourselves comfortable in short order. The R.O. gave us some chocolate and it was then announced that we were breaking camp to advance into a town a few miles further up ahead.

That was fine with us. We had seen enough American G.I.'s that day not to have any qualms about getting a little closer to the front now. We travelled in the panel truck and it started raining again and the roads were quite muddy. We took the liberty of glaring at the German civilians from our armored car equipped with carbines. An overweight German civilian approached us on a motorcycle. One of the G.I.'s ordered him to get off his motorcycle and walk. He looked like he was boiling mad but there was nothing for him to do but obey.

All the good food that I had eaten began to tell on me. I could feel something inside that was not to be denied. I apprised the driver but there was nothing he could do as we were riding in close convoy style. After about an hour of riding there was a sudden halt and out I popped, all ready. We did not stop very long either and it was practically split second timing. I got back in the truck to button up just as it started to roll. I felt much better after that.

It was well after sundown when we got to town and everyone moved into their quarters without any loss of time. They had moved half of the city into the other half so that the soldiers would have enough room. Everybody had been instructed not to touch anything. Nonetheless, a good many felt obligated to liberate some of the chickens and eggs for the outfit. Guards were stationed and a steady watch was kept of the ground and air. We had no objections to that, of course. Russ and Chip slept in the same room while they moved a G.I. out so that I could sleep in another room by myself in a single bed. I crawled into a beautiful feather bed and dozed off in a little while and then awoke during the night. I went out to check up on the guard. And sure enough he knew where the latrine was. I was a little late but such things were particularly unimportant now. The next morning I got a clean pair of O.D. underwear shorts that I needed that Russ still had in his bag.

We got up a little late for the regular breakfast, but we went over to the mess hall and were told by the cooks that they were all through and they certainly were not going to disrupt their schedule just to have us put on the feedbag. We did not care to raise a fuss so we retired quietly swallowing our grief with a half-dozen fresh eggs and trimmings. When the A.C.L.O. (Air Corps Liaison Officer) found out he went back to the cooks and explained it all and they then dragged out some sandwiches, coffee and pie. We sat down near an open fire in a barn next to the G.I.'s peeling potatoes and got acquainted with the latest batch of corn while they worked. I did fine with the sandwiches and coffee. They tasted good the first time. I did not want to take a chance of tasting them a second time. So I took a pass on the pie. Mind you, I was not feeling bad, my stomach just did not see eye to eye with my eyes.

Then a limousine and chauffeur drove up to take us to some other headquarters. They took our names at the hospital near Wurtzberg on April 21 at the 42nd Division Field Hospital—when they examined us verbally. They marked us off with malnutrition and took our pulses and bags. The hospital grounds were very spacious and we had the run of them. Large red crosses were marked on the ground so that there would not be any mistaking them. One of the patients said that a Goon came over every single night at about 11:00 p.m. He vouchsafed that it must be a night-fighter jet job as it had not been caught and everyone knew that it was coming. We could tell we were no longer close to the front. They only brought in one battle casualty right from the field. But even more than that, there were two latrines. One for the men and one for the nurses. Chip and I walked over to the mess hall. Chip promoted some cheese from Cooky. Cooky turned out to be an ex-civilian baker and was making doughnuts. He made two special twisters for us and of course they were delicious. There was a stack of German silverware laying around and Chip picked out a set of forks and knives with the swastika emblem.

The next thing we tried to do was to get some clean clothes but we had to wait another day. Then we got outfitted from head to toe and took a shower so that we could put them on immediately. We went during the ladies' hour and had to wait for them to finish. Some liberated Italian prisoners joined us and I promoted an Italian Star—Army insignia. I had one back at the tent in Italy but I figured that it was long gone by now. After the shower we felt real good and threw our old clothes away. Even as much as we had been attached to them. Russ and I had not permitted them to get wet with soapy water while we were being detained. They did not require too much consideration—after all, they could practically stand up by themselves.

We got a ride to Paris on a C-47 and then an ambulance on 22 April still assigned to the medical corps. The next day I wrote home using V-Mail forms. So my family knew where I was shortly after that. When we got to Paris I weighed myself, after what I considered much more normal eating for the last month or so than for the last six previous months. I felt we were eating so well that there was not any real pressure to leave. I knew we were high priority because we took precedence on leaving before a General and a pregnant WAC that were awaiting shipment home. We saw Shag in Paris. He had escaped twice and then was liberated. He had made a conquest at the top of the stairway. He had gotten a car and ridden it towards the rear until it ran out of gas. He was now with the C.I.C. (Counter-Intelligence Corps) and waiting to be shipped back. He was not going to fly back because the last time he had been in a plane he had an accident.

On May 4th we left Paris and buzzed the Eiffel Tower and then landed at the Azores. The pilot was very concerned with the operation of #3 engine and had it looked at on the Azores. Russ was also very concerned with how the engine was missing and we were not concerned about waiting a few more hours. On May 6 we arrived in New York. There I was assigned to be in charge of a small group of G.I.'s moving from the hospital to the airport. They were all combat veterans and they probably were all waiting to see if I would pull rank being the only commissioned officer. The first time I said "Let's go" they waited. When I said: "C'mon fellows, we have a plane to make" they all started walking. I felt that if I had insisted on pulling rank they still would have obeyed but reluctantly. If I had been in their position I probably would have felt exactly the same way. On May 7 we arrived in Detroit and left the next day.

IT'S A GREAT DAY IN CHICAGO MAY 8, 1945 and on

34/ITS A BEAUTIFUL DAY IN CHICAGO
CHICAGO, IL APR/MAY 1945

Going from Detroit on 8 May 1945 to Chicago, while over Lake Michigan we heard on the airplane radio that it was V-E (Victory—Europe) Day. The next stop for me was Hines Hospital, west of Chicago. Russ went to California and Chip had gone on to his home in Texas.

When I weighed myself again, nine days after weighing in Paris, I had gained twenty-three (23) pounds. Of course, this was due to eating regular meals and not even counting the few days before we had walked through the lines when our diet was so much better than when we were in Langwasser.

When I first returned, there were not that very many social affairs. But their attendance included only a few civilian males. Time moved on and with it V-J Day and mass discharges. Once the gates were opened, everyone was asking everyone else in uniform: "When are you getting out?" It was no longer so fashionable to be in uniform. Now at the numerous dances etc. there were only a sprinkling of uniforms. Army and Navy news now was almost all relegated to the sports pages. It was many months before complaints attained enough mention to put it back on the front pages and then only for short periods of time.

When Arnie first got back we arranged a double date. Everything was going according to Hoyle and we were driving along in the car. After a deep silence Arnie spoke up with: "Gee, I used to know what to say". He had been in for 33 months and had spent 32 months overseas. The first thing he did upon returning was to remark that the natives were very friendly here. He must have gotten back into form soon after that because it was not long before he remarked about a particularly sharp sexy article with: " She had class with a Capital A".

The first letter Burns sent Rudy travelled in distance almost halfway around the world to be delivered less than fifty miles away. They played tag all over the Pacific with Burns usually being a little closer to the lines. Burns' 49th Fighter Squadron with such men as Major Bang and Capt. Johnny piled up the best record in the Pacific and were General MacArthur's honor guard in entering Tokyo. Burns was a Sergeant in the headquarter's squadron. Rudy was in Finance with the 5th Air Force.

Burns had marched into Tokyo behind General MacArthur and got his name in the paper for being one of the first Chicagoans in Tokyo. After a few months of loafing the GI's in his Company got tired of waiting and went to see the High Command about getting home. The Big Boys did not believe their story about having done so much, being over so long and still staying in Japan. So they checked up and then things moved fast. It took ten days for Burns to come from Yokohama to Frisco. After ten more days he got home and took off his uniform. He sent a telegram after he had been waiting a few days at Frisco. Some of the guys with him could not wait and took their own means of travel using their own feet or thumbs.

Rudy had seen Burns only a few weeks ago and was on his way to see one of our sisters to give her the latest news. Rudy was an obliging fellow. When people were convinced that he ought to be nervous after all his war experiences he gave them a very good act of nerves. He complained to me that when he talked to civilians they never fully understood. It took a GI to find out the second and intended meaning. Our sister said that she had to guess at half of what I wrote because of the phraseology.

After wearing the Officers' dressy uniforms for almost two years, I'm finally taking a shine to them. Particularly on the seat of the pants. But talk about someone falling in and coming out smelling like roses . . . that was our old friend Gordy. He came over to Italy just before I got shot down. The first time he came over I had made an emergency landing on Vis and was expected back at the field in a couple of days. The next time he called I was MIA (missing in action). He was stationed further away from the lines than I was. He had some trouble and could not work too hard . . . unless he had to, maybe. He was made Corporal with a sort of floating responsibility on the ground. Never got within a hundred and fifty miles of the front. Admittedly he did take a boat trip across the ocean. He spent one year overseas and came back shortly after V-E Day. Wearing not one or two or even three but seven—mind you—seven battle stars. Of course, it was all official. He got in line a few months later and they let him out. They almost stopped him when they found out that he did not have two years of service.

My old friend, Alex thought he had heart trouble and went to Hines to see about a possible pension. I cracked a cap (tooth) on my bridge, the absence of which glared at people, so I accompanied him. The car stalled in the driveway of the parking lot so we left it there and went in to see what we could have done. They just told Alex not to work out too hard with the dumbbells. The second guy that saw me was much more interested in exchanging experiences than in filling out my form. I finally got to see the dentist who meticulously had me X-rayed and my teeth description noted. He got a fair match of color for the tooth and again meticulously put it on the bridge. All the while he kept insisting that it was only an emergency measure, a temporary cap and he did not know how long it would last. For other emergency measures it was necessary to get the medical records from Washington to show that the need for treatment is service-connected. I finally got him to hurry by telling him that my car was stalled in the parking driveway. I got back to the car just when they were calling the gate for a tow.

I took two bites after getting home and the cap was out. So I went to a civilian dentist who had been recommended. He had been born in Europe. The first day I went there our conversation ran thusly:

"You were in the service?" "Yes."
"You were overseas?" "Yes."
"You were in Europe?" "Yes."
"You were bombing over Germany?" "Yes."
"Did you bomb Augsburg?" "No." I said that because it was true and I also figured the only reason he would ask would be some special sentiment for him. It turned out to be where he was born. Five weeks later I walked out with a new tooth replacing the gap.

Yes, it was a beautiful day in Chicago. The Covenant Club was holding a tribute to Roosevelt. My bro-in-law was chairman of the affair so I naturally sat at the speakers' table for dinner. In going to the Club I was accosted by a Canadian soldier. He had somehow heard that the speaker, Dr. Sachar, was talking on a tribute to Roosevelt and he wanted to hear it. So I asked my bro-in-law who was glad to oblige. Thus Kenny sat at the speakers' table and tacitly insisted on regaling us with his private stock of war incidents. He had lived in Oak Park and went to Canada to enlist early in the War. He had evidently been in both the Air Corps and the Infantry according to his anecdotes. He even happened to have clippings, just by chance, about his exploits. The local papers had given him a few interesting writeups and we all looked at them. He showed us his SS boots he had taken from a German. Telling us that those boys were particularly anxious to get rid of such identifying goods which would then entitle them to "special" treatment.

He got such a special delight out of saying to one of the women: "You've only got one earring on your ear". And as she became alarmed and reached up to check her earrings he would add: "The other one is on the other ear". But the one that I enjoyed the most was the one about a friend of his who had spent a weekend at a resort with an English girl. As they embraced before parting at the train station, she lovingly whispered to him: "You kiss almost as good as those African gentlemen".

As was everyone else upon returning to their circles of relatives and friends, I was bombarded with questions. And with my bro-in-law having such a large circle of friends that knew me, and my sister being such a popular hostess there was not much else to do but invite them all over so they could hear a first hand report of the War. So three evenings in a row they invited about thirty to thirty-five people. When they arrived after dinner we would all adjourn to the living room and sit in as big a circle as we could. I sat at one end and spoke almost non-stop for three hours, each time, with my bro-in-law next to me acting as interlocutor.

We usually started with the mission over Germany when we made a forced landing on Vis to the present. They were particularly interested in the different places I had been, how I felt when being shot at, how the people acted, how the Germans treated me etc., etc. The time the Rabbi came over he zeroed in on my attitude or what I relied on when the flak was bursting around the plane but I'm afraid he did not get very satisfactory answers. He has written a number of good books about religion and I have since become an honorary member of the Brotherhood at the Temple.

By such mass discussions I was beginning to bore myself with my own stories even though I tried to tell and emphasize different things each time. About that time, one fellow I had practically grown up with, James buzzed me and we spent a Sunday evening parked behind the Aquarium and I went over my story again. There were very few of the fellows that I had run around with either still at home or had yet returned home from overseas. But there were still enough of them so that I got a little tired of telling them all at different times. After a few dozen people had suggested it, I finally agreed to write a book. After that it was simple to say that I was writing a book. The only hard part was taking the time and effort to write.

Then if I got too bored of talking about my experiences I would just say that I was writing a book. They could all read it when it was finished. Then everybody wanted me to give them copies. Little did I know what I was letting myself in for by starting a book. Whoever said that success was 1% inspiration and 99% perspiration must have written a book.

One of the advantages of the natives asking so many questions was that those who returned with some bitterness in their hearts had an opportunity to get it off their chests. But it also seemed that the longer it took a GI to return, the more bitter he was on the average. Each GI has his own collection of hardships and injustices to relate about himself and his friends being delayed at coming home.

There is still another aspect of the GI's returning home to questions that I must mention. There is no doubt that the civilians all meant well; it was just that the repetition of some questions become so frequent as to be irritating at times. But one should then come up with an answer that satisfies everyone including one's self. After you have been asked: "How does it feel to be back?" fifty times or more and so many asked it—then what? Rudy would answer: "How do you think?" I liked to startle them when they asked: "Are you back for good?" with: "Well, it ain't for bad." And then most of them would ask: "How was it over there?" They asked stereotyped questions like that without thinking what the answer might be. I think the average GI like myself, wasn't half as much interested in arbitrarily classifying his feelings and experiences as he was in enjoying the more obvious advantages of being amongst old friends and surroundings.

34/EPILOGUE 1995

Some events have come to light since shortly after the end of the war or later. As for instance while waiting in a dentist's office a couple of years after the end of the war, the writer picked up a copy of the Chicago Tribune and read a story on the front page. It was about a gunner, a Sergeant Lawful from Detroit from Phill's crew who had willed a rose a week to a girl in Detroit that he knew. It went on to say that the girl was embarrassed because she did not know the Sgt. that well at all. Also, she was married by then to another person. But apparently he was most impressed by the girl. Sgt. Lawful was apparently the crew chief on Phill's crew and while transferring the flow of gasoline from the tanks to the engines still running had frozen his hands. He was therefore unable to pull the ripchord on his chute and plunged directly to the ground. When this was shown to the dentist, it is most questionable that it was believed.

At one of the reunions, in Chicago, about thirty-five years after the fact, another member from Phill's crew, who was with us on that last mission and also had a number of other problems, and was from Illinois, was still extremely emotionally upset that Sgt. Lawful had not told anybody that his hands were frozen because then somebody could have jumped with him and pulled his ripchord.

Bret came to the reunion in Chicago and we happened to sit at the same banquet table with him and another member of his crew and their wives. They had been shot down also and then they were liberated at the end of the war. He had told his wife all about our fisticuffs while I had never mentioned it to anyone. We discussed a few things about the altercation and I mentioned that he had come out better than I. He then asked: "Who won?" His crew member repeated that I had said that he had gotten the better of the match. However, I did not mention that I had lost my two front teeth because of the trauma, thanks to Bret.

Paul, the pilot, after the war, had finished a tour with American Airlines and retired to the east coast, right on the shore. He has an oceangoing motor boat that is insured only for him to drive. I asked him if he ever got a Private Pilot's License, after I proudly showed him mine. He said: "Yes". He then mentioned that he had a friend who had asked him to take her for a ride and the examination he got for a checkride was most minimal. After all, he had thousands of hours on his pilot log. When he did take the friend for a ride, she had to use a barf bag except that they didn't have any. That was all the private flying he had done.

Peter, the Co-Pilot, when he retired, moved to a retirement development where everything desired is within easy reach. When we visited him and his wife, I asked if she ordered fish when they ate out, as she did when we went out while in the service because Peter did not like fish. I never got an answer. They looked a little quizzical and I did not press the question.

Charlie, the crew chief, who had gone to Yale before the war, finished his college and law school and is now a lawyer and judge on the east coast. At one of the reunions, Charlie said that when Abe flew in our plane as the bombardier, he would curse Hitler when he dropped the bombs.

Gene, (GRHS) the nose gunner, wrote a few times, about

his experiences as a cross-country truck driver and a few of the things he would do to make sure that he collected his past due wages while on the road.

Buddy, (GRHS) the bombardier, is deceased and we have also lost touch with his sister who had moved from the east to California.

Billy, the ball gunner, who got shot down with us and whose legs suffered so badly because of being so crowded in the 40 + 8 boxcars, because he could neither stand, sit nor lie down, lived in Florida. But the Veterans' Administration in Florida would not accept the fact that his injuries were service-connected. When he moved to the Midwest, he had no such trouble getting the medical attention he needed from the V.A.

Walter, the waist gunner, whose parents came from Europe, like mine, lives in the eastern part of the country in basic farming country and has been and still is busy working to this day.

Tommy, the tail gunner, has never attended a reunion.

Rodney, (GRHS) the radio operator, and top turret gunner, loved to raise orchids, passed away recently.

Russ, whose father was a V.P. for American Airlines, with his wife, came to the writer's wedding and met the whole family. But we have not kept in touch since.

Will, the kid brother, wrote an article in A.R.R.L.(American Radio Relay League) a few years after the war stating that we should shoot a radar beam to the moon in order to measure the distance more accurately. After showing it to the rest of the family he finally got to me and said: "Here, Nick, read this, you can understand it". They did shoot radar to the moon about two years after that.

Nothing has been heard from Chip or Pat since the end of

the war but that is not too surprising inasmuch as everyone has their own lives to live and we each put a different value or spin on our experiences.

CPSIA information can be obtained
at www.ICGtesting.com
Printed in the USA
LVHW042321151222
735344LV00004B/181

9 781401 049164